AND THE MONKEY LEARNED NOTHING

SIGHTLINE BOOKS

The Iowa Series in Literary Nonfiction

Patricia Hampl & Carl H. Klaus, series editors

AND THE MONKEY LEARNED NOTHING

DISPATCHES FROM A LIFE IN TRANSIT

TOM LUTZ

University of Iowa Press, Iowa City

910.4
Lut

University of Iowa Press, Iowa City 52242
Copyright © 2016 by the University of Iowa Press
www.uiowapress.org
Printed in the United States of America

Design by Kristina Kachele Design, llc

The University of Iowa Press is a member of Green Press Initiative and is committed to preserving natural resources.

Printed on acid-free paper

Library of Congress Cataloging-in-Publication Data
Names: Lutz, Tom, author.
Title: And the monkey learned nothing : dispatches from a life in transit / Tom Lutz.
Description: Iowa City : University of Iowa Press, [2016] | Series: Sightline books: The Iowa series in literary nonfiction
Identifiers: LCCN 2016010365 | ISBN 978-1-60938-449-4 (pbk) | ISBN 978-1-60938-450-0 (ebk)
Subjects: LCSH: Lutz, Tom—Travel. | Voyages and travels. | Travelers' writings, American. | BISAC: TRAVEL / Essays & Travelogues.
Classification: LCC G226.L87 A3 2016 | DDC 910.4—dc23
LC record available at https://lccn.loc.gov/2016010365

I have not told half of what I saw.
—Marco Polo

CONTENTS

AFRICA

EUROPE

AND THE MONKEY LEARNED NOTHING

ANECDOTES OF THE SUBLIME

An Introduction

I am addicted to travel. Have been since I could wander to the edges
of my childhood suburban neighborhood and get lost in the woods.
Today, when I find myself at a washed out bridge on a gravel road in
the hinterlands of Bolivia or Azerbaijan, I am unaccountably happy.
I have tried, at various times, to figure out why. This book is another
attempt.

The vignettes that follow are tiny stories from my travels around
the globe—following on those in *Drinking Mare's Milk on the Roof of the
World*—tiny stories of encountering people who moved me in some
way, who sent me, sometimes that night, sometimes the next day,
but more frequently months or even years later, to sit at my desk and
write.

The encounters and the hinterlands are related. There is a reason
why being a stranger in strange land is such a frequent trope in our
stories, and the arrival of a stranger in town the beginning of so
many others. The stranger piques our interest, and to be a stranger
is to be an object of interest. Encounter is primed by strangeness.

And this is perhaps why I am impelled toward the end of the road,
to the farthest reaches, to the nontourist itinerary, to the places
nobody else seems to want to be. Even as a teen, I got a thrill from
ending up at the top of a mountain, with nowhere else to go. Or following a coastal road until it just stopped at water's edge, the sea
stretching away with promise and mystery. This year, in the

Guianas—the three countries on the northeast coast of South America—I followed roads into the interior until they ended at a riverbank, as all the north–south roads there do, still hundreds of miles north of the Brazilian border. And along the coast the east–west roads end at rivers, too. The bridgeless rivers that form the countries' international boundaries. The only way forward is by boat. Heaven.

I first saw roads end at water's edge in a drive up the coast of British Columbia many years ago. Just northwest of cosmopolitan Vancouver is Horseshoe Bay, where Highway 99 heads due north and Highway 1 comes to a ferry dock. The twelve-mile ferry ride offers a slide show of stunning views—the steep, pristine terrain rising from the sea as the ferry twists and turns through the strait between Gambler Island and Bowen Island—before arriving at Hopkins Landing. Back on land a two-lane road hugs the coast for fifty miles until it reaches the ferry dock at Earls Cove. (All the town names lost their possessive apostrophes years ago.) At Earls Cove, another ferry waits for the five-mile or so hop to Saltery Bay, a ferry ride even more fabulous than the last, through Norwegian-like fjords, pure sublimity. At Saltery Bay the road keeps getting smaller, until another thirty or forty miles north, at Powell River, it becomes a back road and soon after peters out altogether at Bliss Landing. The only highway that goes further north is now hundreds of miles inland, and the only way to get to it is to retrace your steps. This is truly the end of the road. Bliss Landing indeed.

The French philosopher François Lyotard wrote in 1979 that the age of "grand narratives"—of the march of civilization, of the progress of the race, of the triumph of reason—was over, that instead of such ideological overreach, historians should be telling *petits récits*, little stories, anecdotes, that we should be telling the intimate tales of individual experience and local communities, that we should hew close to the actual, the particular, and steer clear of the general, avoid the global pronouncement. The question of whether the arc of history bends toward justice is not ours to answer, he proposed; the stories of everyday injustice are as close as we can come to comprehending the enormity of injustice and intuiting its future. The smallpox lurking in the blanket, the wailing of the mother over the body of her slain infant, the sniper's finger on the trigger: this is what we can try to comprehend, what we can attempt to represent.

As these examples suggest, this does not mean larger issues are unimportant. The postmodern condition has bred what Lyotard calls an "incredulity towards meta-narratives," but that incredulity has made us more alert and alive to difference, to multiplicity. We doubt the universalist claims of any way of looking at the world and its glorious and horrific history, even as we embrace the abundance of knowledge. In accepting that conflicting views of the world cannot be resolved, we live in a larger world. In assuming that human progress is not preordained, we accept our responsibility for working toward the justice that will always exceed our grasp.

This basic incommensurability between our ideas and our reality is exactly what awakens our sense of the sublime. Our inability to comprehend the endless variety not only of the universe but even of our own small speck of a planet, of our own time and place, even of our own parent or child, and at the same time the inability of the universe to manifest the vastness of our ideas, what Kant referred to as the mind's surpassing sensual experience—this is the essence of the sublime. We can conceive of the infinite, but the universe is finite. We can imagine universal equality, fraternity, and freedom, but they do not exist. The grand narrative occludes the difference between our ideas and our reality; the petits récits insist on that difference. The anecdote is our ticket to the sublime.

My first stab at a title was "If You Meet the Buddha on the Road," based on the old Zen koan. The saying is that if you meet the Buddha on the road you should kill him. Although this has been interpreted in many ways, most people assume that it means something like the Jewish injunction against having false idols. The Buddha represents greatness itself, a greatness that transcends human understanding, and so anyone, whether we meet him on the road or anywhere else, claiming to be the Buddha is a liar, because if you meet him on the road, he is not the Buddha, he is just a man. The original subtitle was "Around the World in Eighty Anecdotes," and besides echoing Jules Verne, I thought it was honest disclosure: what follows is an anecdotal rendering of eighty moments in my traveling life, with no attempt to use them to trace any world picture or any narrative arc. They are what they are, and the moral of each little story, I hope, remains sublimely obscure. Even when I, as the narrator, have an opinion, I hope you find it somewhat untrustworthy.

The sublime—and anyone who is addicted to travel is undoubtedly also addicted to the sublime—does not reside in a thing or a being, not the Sphinx, not the giraffes loping along the edge of the Kalahari, not the Tuareg on horseback on the Algerian border or the gaucho on horseback in Uruguay or the straw-hatted horsemen of Lesotho or the beautiful children of Atitlan in their multicolored crocheted smocks. The sublime happens to us as we try to apprehend the terrible, gorgeous world all around us and fail, and try again and fail, and fail yet again.

And this is why, as Kant suggested, the experience of the sublime begins as a kind of pain before it gives pleasure, why the sublime is always a complex mixture of pleasure and pain. In the attempt to escape our own subjectivity, to meet not the Buddha, but a stranger on the road, to jump the fence of our own understanding—and why else travel?—we apprehend the particularity beyond our ken. And if we pay attention, no matter how it tries to elude us, and succeed, even for a moment, in opening further to the world, we cannot help but find it glorious and disturbing, astonishing and appalling, stupendous and bewildering, pleasure and pain both.

Welcome to this little catalog of meeting strangers, of moments spent being a stranger, and of the sublime.

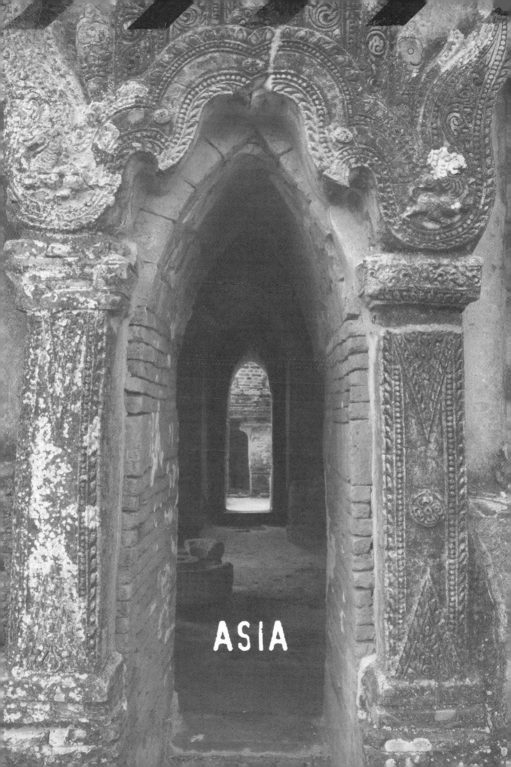

ASIA

THE CHINESE DON'T BELIEVE IN ANYTHING

Kashgar–Urumqi, Western China

Kashgar lies straight east from the border with Kyrgyzstan, some 150 miles, nothing between the dusty border town of Irkeshtam and the outskirts of the old city but empty landscapes of ochre and taupe, a few freight trucks rolling on the two-lane blacktop. Arid, almost plantless, the landscape is a rehearsal for the thousand-mile Takla-makan Desert to follow. After slamming across the extreme, rutted, medieval mountain roads through the Kyrgyz mountains, the road is remarkably smooth, perfectly maintained asphalt. Some scrub brush clings to the almost dry riverbed. Beyond the road and trucks, human beings have left no trace except a single gleaming, jumbo fac-tory complex, complete with dormitories, dropped by Beijing's social engineers exactly halfway between the city and the border.

The old city of Kashgar has a few Kyrgyz in their tall felt hats, a few Tajiks in embroidered caps, but almost everyone else is Uyghur. Next door, the Han Chinese are building a new city, entirely populated by immigrants from the East—part of Beijing's policy to keep the empire from fraying at the borders. Similar cities, called "developing zones," have been built in Urumqi, Lhasa, Jinghong, Inner Mongolia, and other places where China's ethnic minorities live. In most of these places, there is no attempt at urban renewal, no bulldozing of the old city, no attempt to disrupt local cultures, nothing like ethnic cleansing. The Han prefer, instead, to overwhelm. Xinjiang prov-ince, China's far west, is enormous, the size of Texas, New Mexico,

7

Arizona, and California combined, and until the 1950s was almost entirely Uyghur, with a sprinkling of Kyrgyz and others. But Han are now almost half the total population. The new Han city next door to Urumqi is already larger than the Uyghur city and far more outfitted with infrastructure. Kashgar is slated for the same development.

In a café in the old city, one specializing in yak stew at fifty cents a bowl, I asked a cabdriver if the region had changed radically since he was a boy twenty-five years earlier.

Yes, he said. Twenty-five years the Chinese not here.

So you are not Chinese?

He looked confused. We are Uyghur! he said, shrugging his shoulders, arms spread, taking in everyone in the room.

And you are Muslim? I asked.

Of course, he said, matter-of-factly, as if to say, *isn't everyone?*

Do you think everyone in the world should be Muslim? I asked.

Of course, yes, he said, now looking at me suspiciously.

Forgive me, I said, I grew up in a Christian family, most of my friends grew up Christian or Jewish. How do you explain, to someone like me, why I should embrace Islam?

He got hot fast, like a thin aluminum pan over a high flame.

Because there is one god, he said, steaming. And his name is Allah! His anger grew more intense, and he added, almost viciously, and Mohammed is his messenger!

He had gone from calm to irate in seconds, and then, after a few breaths, as we looked past each other, he just as quickly returned to normal. I didn't mention that I found this a not entirely convincing argument.

And the Chinese? I asked.

Jew and Christian know, he said, one god. But the Chinese—and again he heated up, although this time evincing deep disdain, disgust more than anger—they, he growled, they don't believe in *anything.*

The yak stew was rich and thick, just a little gamier than beef stew, and very popular. The place was packed, people sitting close. A happy three-generation family of eight was crammed into a four-person booth with a stool on the end, a plump, red-cheeked baby getting passed around among them.

Two days later, I was some thousand miles northeast, in Urumqi, the capital of Xinjiang province, when fighting broke out. There had been skirmishes between the Uyghurs and the Chinese before, but this was the largest to date. According to official Chinese accounts in the newspapers in the following days, the riots left 197 people dead, the majority of them Han. Uyghur activists claim that more than six hundred died, the majority Uyghur. Mobile phone service was instantaneously curtailed and the internet shut down. No international calls were allowed. Mosques were shut down. A thousand Uyghurs were arrested and hundreds more detained. Eventually, thirty-five received death sentences. Text messaging was restored in the province after six months, but internet service remained blocked for a year. The security services placed forty thousand surveillance cameras in the city. Relations remained tense throughout the region, and in Kashgar two years later, after dozens of deaths in new riots, the Han bulldozed two-thirds of the old city, which had stood for two thousand years along the Silk Road. The official Chinese explanation was that the buildings weren't earthquake safe.

In the Yak Stew Café, as in all businesses, there had been pictures of Han Chinese leaders, but the Uyghur clientele did not seem to notice. I assume the place is now demolished. I had pointed to one and asked the cabdriver what he thought. He looked at it like he had never bothered to see it before.

I also asked him what he thought the future might bring.

Insha'Allah, he said, Allah willing, we will survive.

SEEING THE FUTURE
Seoul, South Korea

Arriving at Incheon International Airport I felt like a kid from the shtetl first seeing New York in the 1890s, or a Hmong tribesman airlifted from the Laotian hills into Minneapolis in 1975. The future lords it over you in the swooping terminal, gleaming, prodigious, awe-inspiring. The subway protrudes into the outsized building as a three-story-high tube of insistent chrome and glass, the front end like an enormous polished bullet. The subway itself glitters with chrome, dozens of TV screens in each car, all showroom-floor spotless. Above ground, the roads are smooth and black, crackless, center lines bright white.

Seoul itself is a mixed bag, with some unreconstructed neighborhoods, a little grime on the older buildings—but even there, the economic vibrancy is palpable. The only real holdovers from the twentieth century or earlier, besides a preserved temple here and there, are the gold hustlers that have an eye out for foreigners and whose mannered friendliness is warning enough. Cranes abound, piling the city higher. "We are very up and coming," a man told me on the subway.

A few days into my trip, also on the subway, I had a chat with a young woman, maybe twenty years old, who said hello, obviously interested in the one foreigner on the train and, like many young people everywhere, interested in practicing her English. She was an odd woman, a little slow to respond when I said something, and it wasn't clear at first whether it was a language problem, or if she was distracted for some reason or on the autism spectrum somewhere. She wore a hodgepodge of clothing items—sweaters and scarves and wraps, all more or less black. I asked her whether she had ever heard of the restaurant I was on my way to, and she said, after a pause, no. I took that as a hint that she was done chatting and opened my notebook and jotted down a few things. After a minute I looked up to see her staring at me. She asked what I was doing, and I said I was a writer—I was just making a few notes about my day.

You are book writer, she said, rather than asked.

Yes, I said. I have one book being translated into Korean.

She looked a little to one side of me, said nothing for ten seconds, and then said, books.

Yes.

When my stop came she had already turned to the door, and I followed her out. As we rode up the escalator, I thanked her for her conversation and said goodbye.

I headed out of the station and noticed she was walking alongside me. I looked over, and she smiled.

You are going this way? I asked.

Yes, she said, and smiled again.

Okay, I said, and scanned the street for my restaurant, quickly seeing it. When we got to the door, I turned to say goodbye once again, and she walked past me, as if I were holding the door for her. I said hello to a waitress in the front of the restaurant, and the young woman talked to her in Korean. She answered and showed us to a table.

I will translate, the young woman said, looking slightly to my left again.

The waitress handed me an English menu and the young woman a Korean one.

I ordered, and the young woman repeated exactly what I said—the names of the dishes were transliterated Korean, and my pronunciation was close enough, which I could tell because she repeated them verbatim.

Are you hungry? I asked.

No.

Do you want to order something small anyway, or we can just share what I've ordered, and a drink?

She turned to the waitress and they had a conversation.

When the food came there were piles of it, and it kept coming. Korean food often has multiple side dishes, and we ended up with twenty or more plates and bowls of various sizes, only some of the food recognizable. The young woman ate with the speed and intensity of a contest eater. She looked up only once, to smile, and then dove back in. Long after I had finished, she was still at it, unrelenting, unconcerned with appearance or really anything but efficient shoveling. It was a remarkable performance, and she was a small person, five feet tall, maybe 105 pounds, maybe less, at least before her dinner.

I tried a few times to have a conversation but got only nods or shakes of her head in response. She was not a student, she did have a job. She shrugged when I asked doing what. Eventually, I quit asking questions and watched. When she was done, the dishes cleared, the check paid, we walked out into the evening, and I thanked her for her help, said goodbye, shook her hand, and started wandering down the street, away from the subway. Once again, she fell into step alongside me.

Do you live this way? I asked.

She took a half block to reply with a shake of the head.

Okay, I said, and stopped.

She stopped.

I said goodbye a fourth time and turned around and started walking back to the subway. She got in step again next to me.

You write books, she said.

I said yes, and started talking about them a bit, until it felt like it had just been a prompt to get me talking. She was not what we call an active listener. For all I knew, she wasn't listening at all.

I decided to try an experiment and didn't say anything for the eight or ten blocks back to the subway. She said nothing. If I looked over at her, she smiled, then looked back ahead. When we got to the station, we went down the escalator, and it was starting to feel, maybe not less strange and unsettling, but funny, like a Mr. Bean episode. I put my ticket in the entry machine, which spit it back out at me, and started walking toward the track.

She had stopped, before the entry, and stood looking at me. I turned and waved, walking backward a few steps, still waving. She waved back, standing still.

I looked back one last time as I turned a corner, and she was still there. I waved. She waved. I walked down the tiled hallway and got on my train. In a minute she was beside me. She must have run.

I asked her what she wanted, where she thought she was going now, and she shrugged, not looking at me.

I'm going back to my hotel now, I said, and need to do some work.

She made no sign she heard me. I looked around the car. It was fairly empty, the day over, and nobody seemed interested in me or us. I wanted some outside read, some sense that this was either as odd as it felt or not.

Getting off the train, I walked with my shadow to the hotel and into the lobby. She followed me in.

Thank you, I said, for accompanying me tonight.

She looked to my left and said nothing. I held out my hand to shake hers, but she didn't lift her arm. I pushed the elevator button. The clerk at the front desk watched us discretely.

Good night, I said, and bowed.

She bowed, almost a reflex, and I backed into the elevator. The bow, perhaps, or perhaps because it was in front of the clerk, had stalled her. She was standing in the same place, looking off in the same direction. I waved as the elevator door closed, but she didn't look up.

As the tiny elevator rose, I wondered whether she'd be there in the morning.

She wasn't.

THE PROSTRATE PILGRIM SLIDES HOME
Jokhang Temple, Lhasa, Tibet

The most strenuous form of pilgrimage in the world begins as a simple standing prayer, after which you lay yourself out full length, face down, kiss your forehead to the ground, and then stand back up where your head just was and do it again. You lower yourself to your knees, fall forward to lie flat once more, and then pull your legs forward and stand back up, moving forward one body length at a time. People in China, India, and Tibet do this around temples, down streets and highways, or overland on rough terrain, sometimes traveling in these five-foot, caterpillar-style movements for a thousand miles, even two thousand miles. An average-size person needs to prostrate himself or herself (almost always himself for the long distances) roughly a thousand times a mile. After a while, kissing the ground with the forehead results in a callus, an enormous crusty, dark callus in the center of the forehead.

Any pilgrimage to the Jokhang Temple in Lhasa, Tibet's holiest site, is supposed to end with three circumambulations of the temple complex, although most people I saw circled many more times than that. Tibetans have a lot of gadgets they use in prayer—the large bronze mounted prayer wheels along the route, which they spin as they pass, or handheld prayer wheels that they keep rotating while they walk or as they sit. There are *vajras* (or scepters), bells, prayer beads, flags, staffs, mandalas—and all of these come in myriad shapes and sizes and styles. The pilgrims and locals buy incense and herbs to

14

keep the four ovens the size of bedrooms continuously fed, sitting at the cardinal points, keeping their protest visible, palpable.

There were men and women of all ages prostrating themselves before the walls of the temple, laying out a small prayer rug for the purpose, staying in one place. Very few circled while prostrating. One man, though, forty-five or maybe fifty years old or so, dressed in traditional garb, was doing his own version. He had special knee and elbow pads rigged up, each of which was padded inside against his joints and clad in sheet metal on the bottom. He stood up, raised his hands in prayer, and then, as if he were diving into a pool or using himself as a bowling ball, he threw his torso low and headlong down the route, flat-out prostrate, suspended on his metal-clad knee and elbow pads, sliding a dozen feet or more on the smooth stones, trying his best not to ram into the pilgrims walking in front of him. When his momentum died, he touched his forehead to the ground, stood up, and did it again. Instead of one body length for every prostration, he made three or even four.

I was fascinated by this man. What kind of spiritual discipline was this? Cheating on the rules, like Penitentes whipping themselves but wearing bulletproof vests so they couldn't be hurt. The purpose of these rituals, I always thought, was achieved by their rigor and dis-comfort. If the rules are not followed, is there any reason to proceed? Can a person take a rosary bead and skip all the prayers and still be said to have performed the rosary? What are tefillin, if not worn on the head or the arm but just stuffed in a pocket? Can a sweat lodge do its work without heat? Is it still a fast if you eat snacks all day?

This guy went around the temple for hours and was there again the next day. There was no questioning the man's devotion; he was rapt, in a state of deep meditative engagement. Of course, people find value in both standard and nonstandard ritual observance, and rap-ture is rapture. But I couldn't figure this one out, this spitting out of the communion wine.

Meanwhile, the five-man Chinese army patrol, with its plexiglass riot shields, strode by on its rounds.

They did not break discipline, at all, even as our gliding pilgrim
. slid past them and jostled one of their shields.

QUIET REPRESSION
Beijing, China

A friend worked for a month at a university in Beijing and found people very welcoming, students and professors, and very helpful as he did what he was there to do, which was to help set up a program in American studies. As part of that, he worked with them setting up a resources page on the university's server, linking to the standard scholarly sites of the day—this was some twenty years ago, and so there was no Wikipedia, and most of what we now know as the web had yet to be invented. Resources were academic, primarily, and available through university servers. He added the available online databases, *Voice of the Shuttle* (the first American studies aggregator), the *Walt Whitman Archive*, and other early forays into digitization.

And then he'd get up and go to the bathroom or go grab a cup of tea, and when he came back, he would find that one or two things he had just added to the page would be gone.

At first he assumed it was a fluke, then perhaps a bit of a programming glitch. He asked around to see if anyone was having similar problems, but they weren't. It occurred to him that his work was being monitored and cleansed of anything considered problematic. He could never see who managed it, and nobody he worked with— they could see his work station and what happened when he was gone—ever let on that they knew there was a problem. He assumed it was the security services, but at what level and whether on site or remotely, he never found out. There was no resisting the repression, he felt, because it was not just anonymous but invisible, it worked by erasure.

When I made it to Beijing many years later, I walked up to a group of students hanging near the entrance of a large park. They were edgy looking, for Chinese students, toward the skater end of the continuum. They were smoking and hanging out in what seemed a slightly rebellious way, given how ordered and buttoned down most people were, their hair a bit longer, their slouch a bit more pronounced, their smoking a bit more insistent. They looked to be taking what amounted to a Chinese walk on the wild side.

They had a little bit of English and were glad to engage—despite wanting to project the universal teenage-cool refusal to seem excited—and they were forthcoming about the state of Chinese society. They scoffed at how slowly China was opening up to the world, they scoffed at the obeisance people still paid to the old proprieties, they scoffed at the opportunities for fun and adventure, at the narrow confines of life as they found it. It made them happy to scoff for me. We were having a good time. Then a man wandered up and said hello, to me and to them, a man of about thirty-five, or twice their age, in a styleless short-sleeved shirt and slacks, and attempted to adopt their posture. He wasn't very successful. The students stopped talking. He looked like the cop he was.

The man said nothing for a moment and then asked me where I was from, where I was staying, how long I would be in China, all with a slight smile, as if it was in fact just friendly curiosity. I answered, and then we all fell silent again. I asked him whether he knew the students. No, no, he said, and they said nothing, made no sign. Was he a teacher? I asked. No, no, no, he said, and then we all fell silent again. It was almost as if he wanted it to be clear that he was a cop. He wanted silence.

One by one the students got up to leave in different directions, and then I did. The man in short sleeves stayed where he was. He looked relaxed, unhurried, unconcerned.

THE GREAT WALL
Mutianyu, China

Approaching the Great Wall is a walk of shame. You wend your way through hundreds of souvenir salespeople, all offering their wares for one dollar. One dolla! Only one dolla! they shout as you pass the booths strung along both sides of the walkway, already steep, approaching the real climb, which is a doozy. And who wouldn't buy a bamboo flute or a metal model of a Xian warrior for a dollar?

Nothing, though, if you try to buy it, costs only one dollar. T-shirts are ten and can be bargained down to six. The salespeople never take no for an answer and always try the old possession-is-nine-tenths-of-the-sale handoff, taking your hand and putting the item in it, stepping back, and demanding payment. The only option is to let the thing fall to the ground, which seems rude—or even cruel if it's breakable—and they know that you feel this. You try to hand it back, and they won't take it. You lay it on the ground at their feet, and that feels rude too. And then, inevitably, you start to get a little pissed—*I don't have to buy this crap! Leave me alone!* Then you feel like a heel. After all, these salespeople can't save up their seven-dollar victories and hop on a plane to the Grand Canyon, and they know it, and you know it. And on in a circle. As soon as you walk away, they shout at the next tourists, One dolla! One dolla!

Some of the entrances have elevators or trams of various kinds to convey you up the very steep hill to the wall itself, but that seems like cheating. The walk of shame is grueling, the climb up is grueling, the climb down is grueling, the walk of shame on the way out worse. Returning through the gauntlet of vendors, now more faux-hysterically insistent than ever, is as socially exhausting as a bad wedding.

But the wall itself is exhilarating. Walking the mammoth snake of rock, it is impossible not to zoom back, to imagine the vast effort—a hundred thousand Chartres cathedrals, all done with crude machines—and impossible not to feel the fear that must have prompted such devotion to the task. At the access points to the parts tourists see (Mutianyu, Badaling, and Jinshanling), the Wall is refurbished regularly, but even in these places, one can walk far enough to come upon the Wall in its eroding state. I felt like a Romantic poet, full of elegiac sentiment, as the seen-from-space crumbling structure wended over hill after hill into the haze on the horizon.

In the middle of the Badaling section, in one of the reconstructed guard houses, an enormous man dressed like Genghis Khan, all patches of fur, weapons, and leather, wearing what I assumed was a fake beard and a jeweled metal headdress, growled threateningly at people, suggesting—although I'm not sure in what language, since it didn't sound like Mandarin or Cantonese, but something animal—that they should get their picture taken with him or die. I wasn't about to descend to what seemed to me the level of the Superman and Darth Vader dress-ups in front of Mann's Chinese Theater, so when he rushed me, I said no thank you. He, like any good Chinese tourist-economy worker, refused to consider my rejection permanent, growling and brandishing his huge curved sword, and I laughed and said, no, look, I'm sorry, I assume you speak some English, so really, it's not going to happen, thanks. In response he growled louder, making no sign that he understood a word. I tried to walk around him, but he jumped sideways, his armor and weaponry clanging, and blocked my way out. I said, no thank you, again, and then translated it in as good an accent as I could muster—*buyao, xiexie*—and tried again to get around him. He wouldn't budge. It was close quarters, every other surface unyielding stone. It was a real sword, and the guy seemed a bit unbalanced. That may have been just part of his Mongol Horde act, it might not have been.

I decided that I'd go out the opposite door and walk that way for a while—there was plenty of wall out there too. As I walked away, I heard, not in his fantastical growl, but in a normal speaking voice, and in an impeccable American accent, maybe with a touch of the Bronx in it: *Cheap bastard!* I swung around, surprised—was he an American? But he had turned and was growling ferociously at some cowering Japanese who he had backed into a corner. I took the opportunity to go out the door I had started for, and as I passed out, I heard, in that same quiet voice, which seemed almost ventriloquized into my ear, *Seriously, you don't have fifty cents?*

Back down the hill, on my way back through the vendors, I bought a few T-shirts and a foot-high statue of Mao.

PICTURE, MAP, TERRITORY
Tokyo, Japan

My map had an image of a Meiji shrine in the middle of a large park, and I walked toward it. It was a hot day, and I worked up a sweat on the steady hill.

A hundred yards into the park I passed under a mammoth torii, an ornamental gate made from two perfectly round and straight tree trunks sixty or seventy feet high, with crossbeams above, the top one sweeping up toward the heavens on each end, the bottom one decorated with three golden disks. How is such a simple structure so powerfully beautiful? Families walked the paths that wound off at random angles through fat old trees. The large temple complex in the middle sat in acutely manicured grounds, and somehow the place was accomplishing what all its details—the stunted bonsai trees, with their every twig redesigned; the perfectly proportioned buildings in perfect relation to each other; the stately buddhas just inside the doors—were orchestrated to achieve: I felt myself lifted out of all trials and tribulations. I felt peaceful, oddly calm.

Farther into the complex, in the largest of the temples, a Shinto ceremony was being performed. The people appeared dressed for a wedding or a funeral and looked like Europeans with Japanese faces, flashing all the symbols of the international bourgeoisie, the designer bags, the Italian suits, the designer glasses, the high-polish shoes, the conspicuously quiet and expensive couture. I watched for a while as the Shinto priests, wearing supersized cone-shaped hats and wizard robes, performed complicated choreography with incense censers, walking this way and that as if even they knew the rigmarole was completely random. Other priests reverently waved prayer sticks in precise, coordinated patterns, jumbo sign language for shouting prayers to dead gods. The rich older men in the front rows looked as if they were drawn there not by religious belief or community but by obligation, and if this was anything like the United States, based on some perceived business advantage. They had fifty thousand dollar watches on their wrists and looks of epic boredom on their aging faces, like Episcopalian CEOs at a church wedding for their CFO's kid.

I walked another ten minutes through the huge park and found an older, smaller temple set off the main path, with a sign in Japanese and English explaining that this was one of the few structures in Tokyo not damaged in the war. Next to it was a meandering rhododendron garden. I strolled through, and in one corner of the garden a wooden wall, shielded from the elements by a small temple-style roof, had a series of pictures, maybe ten by twenty inches, under plexiglass. They were black-and-white, and I assumed they were historical shots. I went over to look at them, stepping from round paving stone to paving stone set in the pebbled paths. Each frame held a photograph, fading from the sun, from Hiroshima or Nagasaki, taken in the first few days after the atom bombs fell, showing square miles of devastation, acre upon acre with but a single section of wall still upright, the waste and wreckage a condemnation.

My belly cramped. I looked around, my focus switching from the garden and temple to the people who were milling about, and noticed that everyone around me was old, each of them old enough to have witnessed the mushroom clouds. I also noticed myself for the first time in hours. I was a big white guy standing among these short old people—and you wouldn't have to be a detective to peg me as an American in my sneakers and shades. I was the lone tourist, standing in the middle of a crowd of atomic bomb blast survivors.

For a moment, I felt a kind of consternation—no etiquette book has a chapter for such situations—and then a pure sorrowfulness, followed by a desire to drop to my knees and say I'm sorry, I'm sorry.

My father, who had fought in World War II, had always said that dropping the bomb was the lesser of evils, that there was no telling how many people would have died if the conventional war had just dragged on and an invasion of Japan was necessary. I think we were taught something like that in school. But seeing the curling photographs of entire cities with all their men, women, and children obliterated, seeing people who might be their few remaining survivors in ghostly perambulation—where were they on those horrible days? working out of town? on a visit or a vacation or at a wedding? These images show what they first saw when they returned: their homes, their children, their parents and grandparents, their siblings and cousins, their neighbors, every person they knew and loved and dealt with every day of their lives, every building, every streetlamp, every storefront, every school and temple reduced to cinders in a blinding flash. Desolation.

Sitting on a bench in the shade of the temple roof, I watched the old people wander through the garden, perhaps engaged in acts of remembrance, perhaps just enjoying the rhododendrons, and realized that there was no way of telling from the way they walked or looked or interacted with each other what they were feeling—immense grief, mild apprehension, nostalgia, anger, nothing? A version of Zen, perhaps, the worst torments and serenest exhilarations alike but momentary spasms of consciousness? I felt a mild rush of some unidentifiable communal emotion and sat, for hours, unwilling to move, and not really thinking. I understood, in a new way, what contemplation meant. A breeze wafted by redolent with the odor of honeysuckle. I sat. A small fountain in a corner of the garden kept up a soft gurgle.

Eventually, I got up and wandered off, not exactly at peace, but my problems and desires shrunk to inconsequence by horror.

Of course the Japanese were themselves famously brutal imperialists, in Korea, China, and everywhere else they occupied. In the 1980s I knew a man who had been a Japanese prisoner of war, a British officer in the famous POW camp that built the famous bridge over the famous River Kwai. Many decades after the experience, he carried an intense, bitter hatred for all persons and things Japanese. He was revolted by everything having to do with the culture, and he took an instant dislike to any Japanese person he met.

I, like most people I know, have the opposite reaction, having grown fascinated by Japanese style. Everything Japanese—every product, every advertisement, every structure, every popular-culture style, every piece of packaging, every bench, every sign—seems metadesigned; form and function both somehow in service to an encompassing philosophical aesthetic. I walked around Tokyo with blissful receptivity, marveling even at things—like the size of my hotel room, the size of my hotel room sink—that impinged on my comfort rather than enhanced it.

On my way out of the park, I stopped in a shiny convenience store and bought a triangle of rice, a nori-wrapped sushi-rice cake with a tiny wad of highly seasoned fish in the middle, and the woman at the cash register showed me how to open it: a single yank not only took off the outer plastic but pulled a piece of cellophane out from between the rice and the sheet of nori wrapping it with origami-like precision. Someone had figured out how to keep the seaweed from getting soggy in the refrigerator. An incredibly simple, yet awesomely complex task, like a wrapper that kept the hamburger off the bun and the pickles and ketchup off the burger until you were ready to take the first bite, all without a square centimeter of excess packaging, all of the reassembly accomplished with the simplicity of the next Kleenex popping out of the box, a ridiculous level of engineering genius applied to this mundane task, and it worked perfectly.

Even people in Japan, too—they seemed to move their bodies through space with precision, with no wasted effort.

The inescapable design, the design-within-an-inch-of-its-life amplifies the science-fictional ambience of Tokyo, the feeling that it exists in a parallel, near-future universe. In the streets of Shinjuku, I saw a bevy of Bo Peeps, a group of girlfriends in their late teens, all in baby-blue or pink frilly dresses, blond or brunette ringlets, ruffled knee socks, some even carrying shepherds' staffs. A group of young men stood on one corner smoking cigarettes and joking with each other, all with their severely styled hair quasi-bleached to a dull off-red, all of them wearing enormous, fleece-lined, Chicago Bears warm-up ponchos. Why? It was eighty-five degrees out. They were sweating. Five girls with Day-Glo hair in orange, pink, and magenta wore some kind of dark-brown version of blackface, with white eyeliner and white lipstick. Whenever one boy in a group had his hair moussed and blow-dried into an enormous '80s do, then all the boys he was with had some version of the same thing, they all wore the skinny ties and suits of an '80s rock group, and all had the same platform shoes. Groups of tutti-frutti-colored kids, boys and girls, wandered by, wearing some unholy cross between Pokémon and hippie fashion, with their hair, clothes, bags, eyeglasses, and canvas shoes all the color of one popsicle or another, twenty colors to the outfit. Each one was different, but just barely. There was something purposely alienating about all the costumes. The brown-faced girls seemed to be projecting "fuck off" much more than "aren't I attractive?" And the boys refused to acknowledge anyone outside their group. I walked through these packs nicely invisible.

Everyone else, though, everyone not in the uniform of one or another youth tribe, was very sweet. People who saw me looking at my map came up to help. As far as I could tell, none of them knew how to read a map. They studied mine, sometimes turning it over or sideways, never able to say where we were.

But they went through the motions of being helpful very cheerfully, finally made a guess, and bowing, invariably pointed in the wrong direction.

THE BEGGARS AND THE KILLING FIELDS
Siem Reap–Phnom Penh, Cambodia

A small, bizarre country, Cambodia's misery proclaims itself immediately. The tiny, bus station–like airport at Siem Reap featured a
lineup of men in different uniforms—army, intelligence, customs,
immigration, police?—a gauntlet for disembarked passengers, most
of whom, like me, were unable to tell who was who from the color
of their shirts or the shape of their hats. I handed the first officer in
line my passport, and he looked up with a hardened face of contempt
and suspicion, a look I would become familiar with. He looked at my
passport as if it was loathsome, flipped through it, then handed it on
to the next guy, who did his version of the same. The next guy had
the pockmarks of severe acne, or perhaps burn-damaged skin. All
had the eyes of killers. These men seemed to know and be addicted to
provoking the fear that only an angry man in a uniform can instill.
I kept thinking of the Khmer Rouge—I couldn't think of anything
else. Was I projecting? These men, unfairly or not, looked to me, as
I stepped off the plane into this new world, like the perpetrators of
genocide, and some of the older ones probably were.

Coming from Thailand, the land of smiles, you know you have
crossed into the land of frowns right away. On the ride into Siem
Reap from the airport, my driver looked miserable. When he honked
to let a motorbike know he was passing, the motorbike driver turned
around and scowled. In Thailand, they turn around and grin—driver,

passengers—they all smile. It's pleasant. In Cambodia, they turn with habitual hostility.

In a country where so many people helped kill so many of their friends and neighbors and family, it is no surprise, I thought. The thing that nobody here can deny is the simple, demonstrable fact that anyone is capable of murder, or at least of being an accessory to murder, at any time.

When I asked the cabdriver whether he had lost family he said, no. Then he said, well, my father, we don't know what happened. He was taken away. So maybe.

And did you ever hear from him again?

No. And my uncle died. And my—how do say, my uncle son?

Your cousin—did the Khmer Rouge kill them?

Yes, cousin. Many cousin. My mother.

He said this with no perceptible emotion. And I would find that again and again. Everyone I asked had lost family members. None of them spoke about it in the languages we might expect—no mourning, no signs of trauma beyond the distrustfulness. They said it as a simple fact—let's see, yesterday I had fish for supper, no, noodles, and the Khmer Rouge killed my mother, and tomorrow is Tuesday. Like that.

I asked a guide at Angkor Wat—who had lost many members of his family—why people didn't seem to be upset, why he didn't seem upset.

My case is not special, he said. It happened to everyone. It was what happened in this life. Look at these walls.

The walls of improbable Angkor Wat, with the enormous trees squeezing and snaking among them, hugging some of them to death, already a movie set before it was a movie set, with friezes of Hindu mythology telling crazy stories of monkey gods, the grandeur and madness of it—yes? I said. Angkor Wat?

You don't think Angkor Wat and these other temples were built without blood, do you? Blood is the way of the world. Blood is the way civilizations are built. America is built on blood, yes?

No, I said, I mean, yes, it was.

And so why should we be special? Why should we be the ones who do not know blood?

I knew all this, but Cambodia teaches the lesson anew and with a certain hideousness. We know what we're capable of, and we know the simple fact that one in every four people in Cambodia was killed during the 1970s, as many as two million in a country of seven and a half million, and we know that that does not happen very often, even in the history of genocide. And because this history was minutely documented and is curated in museums, because the bones are still sprouting from the ground, it is very much alive. And it colors every day. The person standing next to you might bring your sister to an old high school, take her photograph, record a statement, torture her, or just kill her outright, her blood spilled on the floor where you both used to go to math class. Anyone could be the killer. Anyone could be marked for death.

It felt naïve to find this violence revelatory. In Siem Reap, the little town that has sprung up to service tourists to Angkor Wat, one beggar had no lips—I don't know whether they had been cut from her face or blown off or burnt off—but it meant that her saliva was always dripping out of her mouth. A ten-year-old beggar was carrying what looked like a dead or nearly dead eight-month-old dirty baby swaddled in a filthy rag, its head dangling like a broken doll's. A beggar with both legs and both arms blown off—thirty years ago? or two, from the ordnance, rained down by U.S. bombers, still surfacing in fields?—was propped up on a small dolly with a bucket for collecting money. He could take a bill with his arm stumps by scrunching his shoulders together and drop it in his bucket. He looked to be about forty. He said thank you, frowning. The level of misery was deadening.

And seemingly endless. The economy was half dollarized, and local bills came in some denominations worth less than a penny. I procured stacks of the local currency to hand out whenever I came to a tourist attraction because, as everywhere, that is where beggars naturally and rightfully gather, until they are run off by police. And the tourist attractions in Phnom Penh are all ghastly themselves, the main ones being the memorialized killing fields such as Choeung Ek (the most famous of the twenty thousand mass graves in the country) and buildings such as Tuol Sleng, the notorious high school that was one of the most prolific of the 150 execution centers around the country.

Cambodia in 2000 still had almost no infrastructure. The only stretch of paved road I saw, a few miles long, running from Siem Reap to Angkor Wat, had been built by the Japanese in the 1990s to prepare for a visit to the temples by their emperor. In Phnom Penh, the roads were serial potholes, filled with runoff, some the size of small ponds of unknown depth. The only way to get around was hopping on the back of a motorbike and holding on to your driver. Wherever you went—museum, restaurant, hotel, market—when you came out a dozen moto drivers would crowd you and claim to be the driver who brought you there.

Tuol Sleng punches you in the face the minute you walk in. The main room featured a fifteen-by-fifteen-foot map of Cambodia made almost entirely of human skulls. (This was removed in 2002.) The Mekong ran through it, composed of a hundred human femurs. The Khmer Rouge, like the Nazis, were sticklers for documentation, and on walls and partitions thousands of portraits of somber Cambodians hang, photos taken just before they were tortured and executed. Each of the former classrooms is adorned with a photo of an interrogation session that took place in that very room, snapped by the torturers. Grisly, bloody, horrifying black-and-white nine-by-twelve framed photos. In some, the victim is on a metal bed frame, chained down, hacked and bleeding. In the center of each room you visit, the actual bed from the photos sits, its handcuffs and chains still attached to the four corners.

Leaving the museum, nauseous, dizzy, I saw fifty beggars and moto drivers clamoring on the other side of the fence. The beggars were what I had come to expect—missing body parts, vast burns, heads missing parts of the skull—and I handed out bills to twenty of them, while a very loud moto driver, with an obnoxious frat-boy energy, yelled that he was my driver, pushing my actual driver out of the way.

No, I said, quietly, you are not my driver. He stuck one arm behind his back and said, well, give me money, then! Look, no arm! and tucking one leg up at the knee, look, I have no leg! Give me money too! He laughed, hopping around on one foot. The other moto drivers laughed, and oddly, so did the crippled beggars, even the legless ones. I got on the back of my driver's moto as the crowd turned its attention to the next death-and-dismemberment tourist exiting the museum. She was crying. The frat boy yelled at her, Hello! Remember me? I brought you here! And the beggars laughed briefly before imploring her for money.

RED RIVER TRAIN

Hanoi–Lao Cai–Sapa, Vietnam

The train ride up from Hanoi, along the Red River, begins by slipping you down a time tunnel. The rail line is on a miniature scale, the track thinner, the cars smaller than any other trains built since the nineteenth century, and the sleeper cabins give a shabby reminder of the luxury compartments of a hundred years ago, complete with Victorian curtains over the windows, worn lacquered wood trim, brass handles. The train is called the Victoria Express.

The trip is very short as the crow flies. I kept looking at the map, trying to figure out why the train—which leaves Hanoi at 9:50 PM— doesn't arrive in Lao Cai, on the Chinese border, until 6:15 AM, an eight-and-a-half-hour trip. It looks, on the map, like two hundred miles, which would mean the train travels twenty miles an hour. I kept asking myself if that was possible. Were there long waits at stations in between? Perhaps the track curved here and there to catch other towns en route? But no, I could see the tracks on my map; they bend a bit with the river, but it's pretty much a straight shot, NNW, to its goal. Inexplicable.

The train website stated: *With dining carriage not operate frequently, many passengers of this train might feel that they are not fully served compared to what they have to pay.* Okay, you go in with your eyes wide open. And it turns out that, yes, the train travels at twenty miles an hour. Rocking back and forth on the wild, unmaintained track, swaying left and right intensely enough that you don't want it to go any faster—even an extra mile or two per hour might send the train careening off the track and into the river below. This doesn't make for relaxing reading or for easy sleeping, but the dining car is closed, and it is dark, not much to see.

Rolled around by the rocking, I half-slept until first light. At around 4:30 AM I pulled back the curtains and looked down to see a fisherman, in his enormous conical straw hat, lower his slim dugout canoe into the misty river. It was like watching a far-off life in a crystal ball, like seeing what an oracle sees, life slowed down, repeating itself, forever, the fisherman trying to outwit the fish, the most rudimentary struggle, in the dim quiet of the morning, on the ageless river, with the train clacking and jacking this way and that, ignored completely by the old Ho Chi Minh–looking guy in his boat, sparse gray beard and all. Wisps of fog parted elegantly for the man, and it occurred to me that he heard this train every day. Every day, it announced the beginning of his time on the river, the jangling train the metallic opposite of his soundless glide across quiet water.

Two hours later, at the border, we arrived at the provincial town of Lao Cai. To the north, China. To the east and west, the Tonkingese Alps.

Terraced rice paddies are plastered against the steep green walls of the mountains that separate Vietnam and China, making for a distinct kind of sublimity—extraordinary nature transformed by extraordinary human acts. Is there a name for that? The stone walls of New England or Ireland are a less spectacular version, each a kind of picturesque version of the Tonkingese sublime. The rice paddies seem carved by a flawless, enormous sculptor's hand. They follow the contours with the art and precision of an architect's model. Up close, the hill people slog through the mud, mud that is caked on their clothes and smeared on their faces as they work with punishing endurance to replant the rice from paddy to paddy, and things look messy, human, unkempt. But at a distance, they look like a perfection that neither man nor nature could manage alone.

And it isn't just the landscape. Throughout these hills are the Miao peoples, many living not very differently from a dozen generations ago, a collection of tribes that include the Black H'mong, Red Dzao, Flower H'mong, Phu La, Tay, Giáy, Muong—pot-smoking, rice-cultivating tribes, each with its own unique dress culture: the Red Dzao with large scarlet turbans and embroidered pants that stop six inches short of the ankle; the Black H'mong with large neck rings, four-inch hoop earrings, and distinctive black leggings that go from below the knee to the top of the ankle, black tunics and gray vests; the Flower H'mong with their multicolored plaid headdresses and stamped tin earrings. From the time that they can walk the girls wear earrings the circumference of a cupcake, and each tribe finds different places on their smocks and belts and pants to embroider. The men pay less attention to how they dress.

The people in these mountains, especially the deeper one goes into the mountains, ask little of the modern world except that it leave them alone. We moderns don't oblige, of course. Packs of tourists like me come and gape at their astounding particularity. The children beg or try to sell homemade trinkets. Some people offer their services as guides. Some rent out their beds.

They say the real hill-tribe life happens farther into the mountains, where people haven't been corrupted, so I walked along the ridges on footpaths, distant from any road. I said hello to one man who was leaning at his door, and he invited me in. His house had a long sloping roof that reached almost to the ground, and inside a cooking pit was burning, with no chimney, simply a hole in the roof for the smoke to escape. The floor was dirt. The man was very, very stoned, and smoking a large joint. All of a sudden these exotic people started to look like hippies to me, too high to do much but grow some food and keep a fire going, living close to the land and forgetting to build a chimney. They seemed less strange, more recognizable, and at once both more valiant and more pitiful—standing their ground, but too high to secure anywhere to sleep except on that ground.

Nobody, anymore, is untouched, but these hill tribes, whether slaughtering a horse for meat or just going to the local market for a sack of puppies, have managed, more than most, to resist outside mores and the allure of the new. They have kept to their local ways against the forces of convention on the Chinese side of the mountains and the prejudice and imprecations of the Vietnamese on this side. They hold fast, they resist, they observe only their own requirements. As a result they have become novelties in a world shrunk to sameness. As far as I could tell, they didn't care about that fact very much at all.

I bowed to the man as I started to leave, and he bowed back and held out his hand for money.

AWAY FROM THE WORLD
Vang Vieng-Nong Khiaw, Laos

East and south of Luang Prabang—in Vang Vieng, in Nong Khiaw, in Vieng Xai—there are monstrous caves catacombing the limestone cliffs. Tourist destinations now, in the 1970s they were where much of the peasantry—and much of the Pathet Lao—hid from U.S. bombing raids. The chambers are the size of auditoriums, some with fifty-foot ceilings, and although there is plenty of room for the thousands of people escaping the constant bombardment, what could life have been like? Cold and damp, not a flat, level surface anywhere. Children getting lost in the darkness. The sky raining fire outside, the animals—it was an almost entirely agricultural country—either in the caverns with them or blown to bits.

Ever since, the gruesome cluster bombs have continued to surface in field and rice-paddy, unexploded ordnance emerging every day, tearing off children's arms and legs, maiming and killing people collecting scrap metal for a living—an important source of income in the impoverished countryside. Still today, almost a half-century later, the bombs kill or maim a hundred people a year, forty percent of them children.

Standing at the entrance to one of the caves, I tried to imagine that torrent of flame and terror. Two hundred and seventy million bombs were dropped, a planeload every five minutes for nine years. I tried to imagine what these people's removal from the world meant—

leaving the farm, leaving the house to be destroyed, leaving the sun, saying goodbye to all that, and trying to adjust to the new discipline of close quarters, to the dank, cold prisons.

What, I asked a woman taking tickets to the cave, what do people think of the U.S. now? Do they hate us?

No, she said. You don't imagine how backward are people in 1970s. People don't go to school, they stay with their rice and cows all day, they never hear of United States. They never even hear of Vietnam! Or Vientiane, maybe! They are peasants.

But they must have asked who was doing this to them, I said. They must have wanted to know.

One day bombs start falling, she said, and they hide in caves. Then bombs stop and they come out. The farmers here, they still don't know what U.S. is, really.

Her friend, who also looked to be in her thirties, was peeling pomelos, making small packages of the peeled fruit to sell to tourists. She casually nodded in agreement.

But the Pathet Lao, I said, they knew. They were supported by Vietnam, they were fighting the U.S. And the Hmong knew, they were fighting for the U.S.

Yes, but, look—she pointed to a passel of kids nearby, playing with a soccer ball—everyone born after those days. Nobody think about U.S. except tourists. Hmong gone, live in U.S. now.

It is true that many Hmong were slaughtered by the Pathet Lao after the war, and many were evacuated. And it is true that half the population of Laos has been born since 2000, that with a life expectancy still hovering around sixty, only a tiny percentage of people who were adults during the bombing are still alive.

Yes, Hmong in Minneapolis, she said.

Wow, I said, you know Minneapolis.

No, she laughed. But I am not peasant. I am businesswoman. Otherwise I don't know. Tourists come to caves, so I know U.S. But my village, Phac Lac, no people see U.S. people. No tourists. Old men in my village? They no hate U.S., they hate Vietnam people.

This made sense—the Vietnamese were in conflict with the Laotians for a quarter century after the Americans left.

And you? I asked.

I was born after no more war. Everyone born after no more war.

THICK AND THIN CULTURE
South Kuta, Bali, Indonesia

To get to the Ulawatu sea temple, perched on sheer cliffs at the far
western tip of South Kuta, the peninsula that hangs off the bottom
of Bali like an engorged teardrop, one has to climb a couple hundred
steps up a steep slippery slope. The forest keeps the path covered
from the sun, but the heat and humidity make for a sweaty trip. As
anywhere in Bali, there are many tourists, but the locals live their
lives without taking much notice. Two parallel communities—it
feels like a conceit, in fact, like a story by Aimee Bender or George
Saunders—two completely separate realities that unfold in the same
space, the inhabitants of the two worlds crisscrossing each other's
paths and seeming not to notice, each in a fundamental way imperceptible to the other—or if not imperceptible, seen by the other as
something like plants or like scenery. Or like the monkeys, that is:
sentient creatures of another species who think and act in recognizable but fundamentally different ways.

The monkeys, who sometimes seem to outnumber both tourists
and locals, don't care about either. For the locals, the tourists are
more or less pests; for the tourists, the monkeys are. So three parallel
universes: on one end of the scale, the ultracultured Balinese; in the
middle, the deracinated tourists; on the far end, the horrible monkeys.

The main difference is speed. The Balinese walk slowly, the men
keeping their stride short enough not to disturb their sarongs, the

women usually chatting, equally relaxed. Being in a hurry would be rude. The tourists walk faster and hike up the steps with purpose, sweating buckets. The monkeys are geometrically faster again, bombing through the trees.

The stone steps up to the temple are just barely wide enough for two people to pass here and there, but otherwise it is a single-file climb. I saw, from the tourists coming down, that it was more frightening in that direction, as too-steep stairs usually are, like going down a ladder the wrong way. A group of six Balinese were going up together, four of them like pallbearers, carrying a small float of sorts, a bier, I guess, since there was a dead pig on it. Dead as in not yet cooked. But like everything in Bali, it had been rigorously elaborated for ceremonial purposes, all its fur scraped off, cut neatly into pink parts, the parts then nailed back onto the float, the head on the front, the forelegs on the sides, pointing straight forward, the hind legs pointing straight back, the pale, rubbery, hairless pig flying like Superman. The rest of its body was in slices. And in between, on top, and on the sides were teetering baroque arrangements of fruits and vegetables, punctuated by hundreds of flowers and seedpods and ribbons. On the back, between the two carrying poles, was nailed its curly tail. A bright, colorful, flying holiday pig being walked up the hundreds of steps like a pasha in his palanquin, undoubtedly as part of some ceremony for that day.

Not a day goes by in Bali that doesn't see a festival, a parade, a ritual marking something on the annual calendar. I wasn't sure what the pig was for, and I didn't ask. I had found, joining a parade here and there, that most people were not entirely sure what, specifically, was being celebrated.

There was no way to pass the float, and so I slowed to a Balinese pace, and that was when I discovered the wisdom of it. I began to cool down, to sweat less, to feel a breeze. I wish I could say I learned this lesson in a deep way and took up slow walking. But I didn't.

At the top of the cliff, the temple was stuffed with offerings, and whatever was happening was not on a timetable. People came and went, not at any perceptible break in the action. I sat in the temple and sang with the people for a while, obviously without any of the words, but it was a mumbling group, and a lot of them were either doing what I was doing, following along, or just not enunciating at all. I then got up and walked the perimeter of the temple, and it occurred to me that from nowhere on the grounds could one see the ocean, which surrounded us on three sides. I sat for a while again on the floor with the singing celebrants and then walked back to the top of the stairway, where there was a viewing point, a place to see over the jungle, down the almost-sheer cliff to the sea. The sun was just starting to get low, and several tourists leaned against the rail and relaxed. The woods were full of monkeys.

I have to pause to say that I hate monkeys. Yes, they are fascinating to watch, but they are sociopaths, like particularly nasty juvenile delinquents—who else would threaten bodily harm for no particular reason? Who else would actually throw their own shit at you? On the way up the stairs I had watched as groups of them surrounded a couple of poor tourist suckers who had bought bananas at the stand below to feed them. The monkeys, like monkeys everywhere, were instant gratification hooligans. Unwilling to have bananas handed to them one by one, they weren't satisfied until they grabbed the entire bunch or scared the holder into dropping them. Then they'd run off and fight viciously with each other over the spoils.

Leaning against a stone wall were a dozen or more of us tourists, and the monkeys had focused on a German man in artistic, expensive, designer glasses, the kind of glasses an architect or a modern art museum curator would wear. He had his bananas in a pack, protected, which was driving the criminal mob of monkeys crazy. Showing off for his party a little, the German held out one banana. A monkey swung by to grab it, and the man pulled it back—a fun game, the humans thought, and laughed. A few missed swipes and then one of the monkeys figured out how to come up on his blind side and make off with it.

The man, ready for the next game, pulled a fresh banana out of his pack just as a mature male swung by. As the man pulled the banana aside like a toreador, the monkey paid no attention and grabbed, instead, for the man's glasses, deftly pulling them off his face and retiring to a close branch. He stared back at the man, holding the glasses in one hand, as if pretending he was going to put them on. These glasses were not just expensive, the man needed them—he was clearly panicked and blinking. He offered a banana and to show good faith at the start of negotiation, two bananas. The monkey knew that a bargain was being made, and he lucidly understood his advantage. He backed a little farther away, made a show of gazing skyward. There would be very many more tourists with bananas in his life. He was the only monkey with the German's glasses. He was way ahead in this game, and he was in no hurry, enjoying the taunt, considering his options.

The German took out his whole bunch and held them forward, gesturing toward his glasses, talking the monkey through the deal—here, the bananas for you, the glasses for me, and the monkey looked from the bananas to the glasses, the glasses to the bananas, and came forward. The man reached for his glasses, but the monkey held them away, motioning for the bananas. The two of them moved slowly, inch by inch, toward the exchange, toward the mutual hand-off, like trading spies on a bridge, and then, just as they were at the creation pose, their fingers almost touching each other, the monkey shot out his free arm and grabbed the bunch of bananas. The German swiped at his glasses but missed, his friends holding him so he didn't fall off the cliff.

The monkey pitched the bunch of bananas under one arm and perched on a branch directly over the smashing sea a hundred and fifty feet below. He took a long look at the glasses in his left hand, looked at the German, who was now pleading with him, almost weeping. And then, after one more long look at the glasses, the monkey turned, stared the German right in the eyes, and tossed the glasses casually over his shoulder, so they floated down the cliff, buoyed by updrafts, before disappearing, finally, hundreds of meters below, into the crashing waves.

Monkeys, I realized, then and there, are not incapable of culture. The complex reasoning that went into that monkey's act, its memorializing of the German's affronts, the flourish with which he let the man know that he was considering both available options, the way he not only got his revenge but represented it—monkeys could do it, they could build a culture, maybe not as elaborate as ours, and definitely not as intricate as Bali's, but they could manage a culture. They are simply too deeply sociopathic to do it.

As an anthropologist working in Bali, Clifford Geertz came up with a method he called "thick description." Previous anthropologists had tried to make ethnography into a science, he said, but this was a technocratic dream, a materialist fantasy, ridiculous, and we can no more objectively catalog the varieties of human experience by charting out kinship systems and burial rituals and grammars than we might fathom the workings of a venomous monkey's brain. We anthropologists, he said, we are bad scientists, fake scientists, but what we have always been good at, what we can be better at, is providing a compelling, nuanced, that is, thick description of another culture. We do it the way we have always done fieldwork—we sit and watch and learn, and we take copious notes. Then we do our best to write it up.

When I read Geertz as a graduate student, I imagined an ethnographer trying to write a thick description of my community, and there seemed to be some magic necessary, like the magic Henry James had, or Edith Wharton—Geertz could go on eloquently for pages about simple daily activities, and like a great novelist, make them redolent of larger meanings. But being in Bali, where every house gets further adorned every day with posts and ribbons and fronds and fruit, where parades with music and banners and flags mark every occasion, no matter how small, where altars are everywhere and are each redecorated every few hours, where offerings are made to spirits on the streets, on walls, in alcoves, where even a pig can become a very temporary but extravagant work of art, where even the monkeys come close to having a culture, perception itself is thickened. I stood looking out at the sea and felt that Geertz was cheating somehow. It wasn't the description that was thick, it was the culture.

The German was upset, of course. He was on vacation now without any glasses, and he had just lost hundreds of euros and his dignity, and he had probably forever joined the ranks of us monkey-haters.

The monkey learned nothing.

I had learned the value of slow walking, but I couldn't practice it. By the time I was back down the steps to my car I was dripping sweat, even as the evening breeze had risen and the sun had nearly set.

HUMAN TRAFFICKING IN SINGAPORE

Over the Indian Ocean

They were not supposed to get married—he was ethnic Malay, she was Chinese, and both of their Singapore families were horrified. They laughed about it. I asked them if they thought they were postracial, a term I was hearing in America. They laughed and she said, We must be!

They worked together, securing laborers for factories. In their thirties, they had no desire for children, liked their work. They hired, they told me—or arranged for various companies to hire—twenty thousand people each year, maybe more. Singapore has a population of a million and a half migrant workers, and there is a constant need for new bodies. Construction workers, domestic workers, and factory workers—the total for each kept increasing, and older workers, burnt-out workers, workers overcome with homesickness, all needed to be replaced. My couple specialized in the factory workers.

Yes, she said. We have one main client, frankly, for whom we do almost all our work.

Although, the man said, we have a very good reputation from our work with them, so other clients ask us to find fifty workers for them, or a hundred workers, and we do that too.

And that is why you are going to Chennai? I asked. I had met them on the plane. I had upgraded to business class with miles; they flew it as a matter of course. They always habitually sat in two aisle seats across from each other; they hated to feel boxed in, they said. I was at the window.

Yes, she said. We go there to hire Tamil workers.

Only Tamil? I asked. It made sense, Chennai is the capital of Tamil Nadu, most of the people there are Tamil, but not all, of course.

Yes, only Tamil, she said.

And then you fly somewhere else and hire workers there?

No, he said. We always hire Tamil, always Chennai.

I must have looked perplexed because he immediately explained.

They are the best workers, he said. We have a reputation for bringing our employers exceptionally good, very reliable workers, and everyone thinks we are recruitment geniuses, but really, we just bring Tamils. They are the best workers, especially in factories.

They smiled at each other, amused yet again at how easy their job was.

And so they come for months? or years? or are they immigrants?

No, they are migrant workers, they are not immigrants, she said. Very different category.

So how long do they stay?

Well, he said, of course employers like them to stay forever, because it costs to replace them—they pay us, they pay travel for the workers, they pay for visas. Most stay about ten or fifteen years.

And why Tamil again? I asked, although I had already guessed—I had images of the Tamil tea plantation workers I had seen in Sri Lanka, steadily working through the rain.

This is a special kind of work, she said. These workers, they come, and they live in factory housing, and they get up in the morning, are fed breakfast, and then take a bus to the factory. They work all day—they are fed lunch at the factory—and then they work, and they eat dinner at the factory, and then they work, and then the bus brings them home to the dormitories, and they go to sleep. The next day, the same. Not everyone can live like this.

But the Tamils can, I said.

The Tamils are the best! he said.

It sounds miserable, I said.

Yes, that is why we would not hire you! they laughed, in a good-natured way. But this is a very good life for the Tamil. That is why they stay so long.

The flight attendants were serving us our business-class meal.

But can they live somewhere else if they want? Besides the dormitory?

Well they could, but then they have to pay for housing and transport, so nobody does it, he said.

Yes, when they do try it, she said, it usually doesn't work. So, no, almost never.

But they aren't prisoners, right, they can leave the dormitories whenever they want?

Yes! Of course! she said smiling. This isn't the gulag!

The flight attendant asked what we wanted to drink. Red wine, I said, thanks. They asked for Cokes.

But the funny thing, he said, pushing his food around with a fork, they don't ever go out of the dormitories. First—he held up his finger—they are tired, and they need to get up early. And second, he said, holding up two fingers and smiling, they don't!

They are Tamil! she said.

THE SILENT RETREAT
Chennai, India

Shanti got up as we were finishing our breakfast to go to the bathroom.

Well, now we will at last have a chance to talk, Louise said. There had been an increasing set of bids for my attention since we met, collecting our baggage at the Chennai airport the night before, part of a minor struggle between them that had started long before, I suspected. As not infrequently happens in this Lonely Planet world, we found, Shanti, Louise, and I, that we were staying at the same hotel for the night, and we shared a cab. Now we were sharing our hotel's breakfast.

Waiting for the bags, in the cab, and during this extraordinary meal of idli, vadai, and upma, all new to me, the women talked over each other, making non-sequitur observations in the middle of each other's sentences, Shanti launching into a new story in the middle of one of Louise's—after all, she knew how the story ended—and vice versa. I would try, by moving my head, to regulate the traffic flow, with marginal effect. I'd look directly at Louise, the sixty-four-year-old from Portland with a Polish accent, and nod, managing to slow down but not stop Shanti (not her given name), the forty-eight-year-old from Bolinas, for a few minutes. Then I'd turn to face Shanti and give her equal time, ignoring Louise's various border raids for my notice, and then, when she had finished—not what she had to say, because that eventuality seemed never to come, but when she finished an anecdote—I'd turn to Louise for a while. They were journeying, together, they told me, in near unison, to the ashram of a most amazing, saintly amma, for a weeklong retreat of total silence.

Shanti excused herself to go to the loo, and Louise spent most of the time she was gone telling me what a wonderful person her friend was. She told stories of Shanti's generosity, her wisdom, her extensive knowledge of the Vedas and Upanishads. What a superb friend she was. How thoughtful and smart. They were both sweet and well-meaning, and although I had trouble imagining them silent, they were clearly devoted to their spiritual practices. They were both particularly knowledgeable about the nineteenth-century mystics Sri Ramakrishna and Swami Vivekananda, and talked about them like they were neighbors they had left back home just last week. They had traveled together many times and had been to India together too—yes, Shanti chimed in, retaking her seat, this was their fourth visit together.

We were about to go our separate ways, but first Louise excused herself for a moment and headed toward the bathrooms herself.

At least now I can get a word in edgewise, Shanti said, rolling her eyes and smiling at her friend's irrepressible chatter. She is quite wonderful, Shanti began.

HINDU, MUSLIM, FISHERMAN

Mahabalipuram, India

On the east coast of India, south of Mahabalipuram, I got out of the
car and took a walk on a largely deserted beach. The sky was gray
and threatening, a bit of breeze coming onshore. There was some
plastic junk here and there on the sand, and a cluster of fishing boats
a few hundred meters south. A guy selling seashells approached, and
we started talking. He lived in the fishing village whose boats I had
noticed. The village, like Jerusalem, is split into religious quarters, he
explained, with Catholic, Hindu, and Muslim sections, and—and this
was a new one on me—a section for Fishermen. I had heard the Fishermen described by a cabdriver who took me to a beach near Chennai; he wouldn't let me get out where the Fishermen lived because
they were too dangerous—and it didn't occur to me right away that
he was talking about a caste, not just an occupation. But then he
went into a rant like Strom Thurmond in the 1950s—the Fishermen,
he said, are terrible, they are lazy, evil, they fish in the morning and
then give their catch to the women to sell and drink and play spades
for money all day—and it started to dawn on me.

They make money, the cabby had said, shaking his head. But don't
use correctly. The women, they are 70 percent decent but 30 percent
of them are indecent, and their husbands kill them and they go to
jail. They don't use money correctly.

The seashell salesman also warned me against the Fishermen.

Listen, he said, I tell you, don't talk to anyone, let them talk to me, and I will talk to you.

Some women walked by and I asked him whether they were Hindu or Muslim—assuming Hindu because they were in classic saris. He was shocked at my ignorance.

Fisherman! he said, meaning, *what, are you blind?*

He took me into a school in the Catholic section that had a chapel with some crypts of Portuguese who were buried in the early nineteenth century. The schoolyard was filled with a thousand little kids who swarmed around us, laughing, and saying hello and wanting to shake hands. Some gave me a smack on the butt while I had five or six on each hand like an inverse Shiva, a bizarre raucous pied piper scene, all the boys and girls in their uniforms, hundreds and hundreds of them shouting, Hello, in English-lesson style, what is your name?

Then we went on to the Muslim quarter.

This is Muslim temple, the man said.

The building was the size of a bedroom, but with a couple of minarets. Goats and cows wandered through the streets.

I asked where he lived, and he didn't exactly say. He said his house was made of woven reeds, so it was washed away by the tsunami. Many houses in the village were gone. He pointed to another small building.

This Hindu temple, he said, has cobra guards, we can't go in.

He was apparently serious. A little farther on he stopped in front of a third building.

This Fisherman temple, he said. Female god.

The beach in front of this temple had a hundred fishing boats pulled up onto the sand and the wreckage of another fifty, some split in half, some just skeletons, scattered around. I wondered if they were used for parts. In the marshy area between the town and the beach, more goats and a couple of cows grazed knee-deep in the tide pools. Packs of dogs roamed the village streets and the beach. Jetsam, mostly plastics of various kinds and colors, had been raked into nasty piles by tide and wind.

A couple of Fishermen walked by. They looked downtrodden, didn't look up, clothes ragged and dirty. They didn't say a word to me. They didn't want anything to do with us.

WHERE IS YOUR FAMILY?

New Delhi, India

At a large plaza in New Delhi, at sunset, crowded in that very Indian way, thousands of people in a public space, children running around, enormous families sitting in clumps together, and young people walking and talking in threes and fours, yet for all the bustle and all the flesh, it managed not to feel too crowded or claustrophobic. I think of being at an outdoor rock festival and that panicky feeling that I'm about to step on someone or be trampled myself. For whatever reason, in this enormous red stone pavilion, sharing the evening air with thousands and thousands of Indians, I had none of that fear.

Child after child came to me asking to have their picture taken, small kids, teenagers, whole families. It was as if I was making balloon animals or performing with puppets. We would look together at picture on the display screen, and they were happy, grateful—I was providing some kind of service, I realized, and of course happy to do it, even if I didn't entirely understand. After a snap, the subjects and then another dozen take a look, and for all the traffic around the tiny screen, there is almost no jostling, much less pushing. I am in a crush of bodies, and it feels not like an invasion of personal space, not like a rude intrusion, but like family piling on a couch to watch TV, or a sports team huddling up. We're all in it together, and we feel it. When a family comes together to get a picture, cousins and aunts and uncles and nieces and nephews come running and hug their way into the frame. Where is your family? a boy asks me, and I say America. He looks confused.

Something similar happens on the trains, although it's less personal. Indian passenger cars are like subway cars—most people stand. And they are extra wide, much wider than trains anywhere else I've been. At every stop a few people get off but many more get on. Eventually, you think, uh-oh, that's about capacity, we're all very close to each other, maybe the next stop is that one where everyone gets off. But no. The car is full, but a hundred new people get on and only ten exit. Like a sophisticated machine, everyone adjusts an inch. Calmly, automatically, the air between each of us is narrower. It doesn't matter, we're fine. The next station, it happens again. It seems we could not sardine it any further, but we do, and nobody gets aggravated, nobody panics, nobody even seems to notice. We are all a self-regulating system, like atoms with the negative and positive charges making for equilibrium, we suspend each other, we get closer, and it's kind of beautiful.

The American newspapers have many stories of stampedes and rapes and religious violence, but India is remarkably peaceful. Violent deaths are 25 percent lower than in the United States per capita, half what they are in Thailand, the land of smiles, a quarter of the rate in the Philippines.

Reading the American sociologists, you'd expect this enormous mass of humanity to suffer from alienation, from anomie, you'd assume that the feeling of being a single atom in so vast and anonymous a crowd would make people lonely. But very few people in these crowds are alone. Large families move across the square more or less together. The oldest move the slowest and form the nucleus, the youngest kids run away and circle back, the teenagers wander off for some privacy and wander back. Groups of same-sex friends—not two or three as we are used to in the states, but eight and twelve, walk together or lean against a wall. The lonely wanderer in the crowd is the exception. It is why people find my solo travel so baffling. Why would someone with resources make that choice?

At the plaza, as the sun is disappearing, the fourth person that day asks me where my family is. And I can see, when I say they are back in the United States, that like the others, he pities me.

THE OIL OF THE LOTUS PLANT

Mysore, India

The boy touts in the Indian cities are very impressive. In Mysore, one insinuated himself so skillfully into an impromptu gathering in a side street—I had ended up photographing an extended family outside their front gate—that it took a while to realize that he wasn't really part of the group. I had been taking some pictures of a ten-year-old girl and her six-year-old brother. She was very sharp, and clearly a wise guy. She had more English than her older sister or mother, more than the rest of the clan that promptly gathered as I loitered, snapping away. One of her aunts—I'm guessing at these relationships since the English was very limited—loved the camera and wanted dozens of shots of herself, one holding each of the available babies.

Canada? the ten-year-old asked, or maybe she was twelve.

No, America, I said.

She rolled her eyes, as if to say, *we established that already.* Yes, Canada?

I've been to Canada, yes.

She put her hands on her hips, disgusted with adult stupidity in the way only a girl that age can manage, and tried once more.

Yes, English, yes, America, she said, then, emphatically: *Canada?*

I hadn't noticed the boy arrive. He was around thirteen, I guessed, with the look of a good, obliging student, and he wasn't as camera-crazy as the rest. She wants to know, he said, if you speak Kannada, the language of Karnataka, where you are.

The girl looked at me and wagged her head, like *what did you think I was asking, dummy?*

A few more family members came by, I took a few more shots, the aunt found another baby, but then I started to say goodbye and began walking away. The boy followed.

Listen, he said. Can I help? I have good English, and I know many interesting things about the city.

Okay, I thought—interesting, a little tout. Sure, I said, like what?

Right here, in one block, he said, is a man who makes cigarettes, very interesting.

Sure, I said, since it might, in fact, be interesting. We went around the corner, and then he stuck his head in a dark, basementlike room. He hopped in and came out a long minute later. It's okay, he said, you can go in.

After you, I said, and once he ducked back in, I took a look and saw a man sitting on the floor, indeed making cigarettes.

Please, come in, he doesn't mind, the boy said. I stepped in the dark room and exchanged hellos with the cigarette maker, who looked very stoned, and watched as he very ineffectually rolled some small cigarettes on a tray. The tray had a pile of hand-rolled cigarettes on it, all of which looked better than the misshapen things he was managing. I'm not sure what the con was, but I thought okay, that was interesting, and popped back onto the street.

Would you like to buy some cigarettes from the maker? the boy asked. This is usually what tourists do, to help him a little. Just retail price. I said fine, and the price was reasonable, almost, so I bought a few.

He handed them to me, and I looked at them and said, I'm glad you gave me the cigarettes the real cigarette maker made. That guy in there—his were terrible.

Most tourists, he said, they can't tell. That is the cigarette maker's brother. He does other work.

Yes, I'm glad he does, I said. What's next?

This made him reappraise me; I'd caught him in a con and was ready for more.

Ah! he said, in recognition, looking me in the eye. There is a man I would like you to meet. He is, like you, very educated and intelligent, and I think you would enjoy meeting him. He also sells essential oils—you know essential oils? Only the best, because he is like a chemist, he is very good. But you will like to talk to him. Do you like philosophy?

Well, I said, in fact, I do! Let's go.

Along the way he kept up a patter, and we wound through the city, multiple turns through small streets, and I had completely lost track of where we were. But I could just grab a tuk-tuk anywhere and get back to my hotel, so I was far from worried. All of the standard questions—why are you not in school?—he had the obvious answers for— it is a teacher training day—and he almost seemed disappointed that we had to work through them; he had expected better of me, and I was losing rank quickly, slipping back into being a generic mark.

We reached the essential oil philosopher's place of business, and he greeted me with a high Oxonian accent and impeccable manners, refused my refusal of a cup of tea and had the boy run out after some. He grandly ushered me to a chair in his office, which looked like a Hollywood art director's notion of the study of an eccentric Oxford don in reduced circumstances—piles of books and papers, overstuffed filing cabinets, some fetish objects of indecipherable origin, all of it looking like it might have been through a fire. On his desk, among more stacks of papers and books, were a line of small, irregularly shaped bottles, containing liquids of different hues.

He was over six feet and looked a bit like the actor Geoffrey Rush, although radically slimmer, younger—about forty or forty-five, and, of course, Indian. When speaking he used his hands with a regal air, and he spoke constantly—looking conspiratorially at me in the places where I might be expected to say something while holding up his hand, giving me almost a wink: *Wouldn't it just be easier to relax and let me continue? Let's not stand on ceremony!* And then he would launch into his next set piece. He was quite lucky to have attended, he let me know with exaggerated humility, St. Catherine's College, Oxford, on a Commonwealth Fellowship.

Quite an extraordinary thing, of course, for a boy raised in an orphanage in a third-tier Indian city like Mysore. Yes! Don't say otherwise—I wasn't about to—it is not much of a city, but the orphanage, I'm happy to say, through the efforts of some of my classmates and I daresay some efforts of my own, you won't mind me saying, is now seeing much better days. There is yet strenuous work to be done, of course! I try to volunteer once a week when my schedule permits, as it gives me such intense pleasure! Believe me, I know how fortunate I have been—Ah! Here is our tea!

He went on like that nonstop for thirty or forty minutes, segueing quite naturally into the medicinal and alchemical powers of essential oils and starting to dot examples of them on my wrists and arms and forehead, giving me the scriptural and scientific pedigree of each, the chemical properties of the various botanical substrates, the curative properties and narrative testimonials of people he had treated with each. He had been very interested to note, while at Oxford, he said, that a kind of naïve radical empiricism had made it impossible for Westerners to appreciate forms of knowledge long understood on the subcontinent and, of course, not just here, but across Asia and elsewhere. They were unavailable to Western science *by choice*, which is the height of intellectual irresponsibility, he didn't mind saying. Every once in a while I would throw in a question, ask about a scholar or writer, and he was exceptionally nimble, fielding everything with a bit of a silent laugh.

Yes! he said at one point, I do so *miss* this kind of intellectual discussion, which is why, peradventure—he said peradventure—I am *so* glad you have come by—anyway, he went on, and on, and it was a bravura performance. I didn't buy an iota of it: not the orphanage, not the Oxford, not even the oils—his laboratory he would love to show me, he said at one point, it was just a forty-minute walk—no he didn't suppose I had that kind of time.

Eventually—when, I wasn't sure—he realized that I wasn't buying his act, that I was in effect playing him as well, and then we entered a new zone, the emerging theatrical compact being that I was now to buy the quality of his performance as performance, and he would do his best to give me some dramatic twists and turns—was he over-playing his hand? Never! He was just teasing me!—would he fumble the final task? No! He would box me in rhetorically and somehow extract the maximum payment.

An hour later, he had decanted five dollars' worth—and he was categorically correct, that was the absolute maximum he could have extracted—of his most significant and potent oil, lotus oil, into a tiny vial, which he then handed to his young assistant and tout to wrap for me—we wouldn't want it to break or leak, he said, when I suggested that wrapping wasn't necessary. Let the boy do it properly, he said, lowering his voice to a just-between-us timbre, you know it is so important that we train these young men to the right standard. The boy ran off somewhere to wrap the vial and quickly returned.

You will be astounded by the effects of this oil! the man said. My goodness, I hope you will return and let us know. He never for a blink broke character and ended by suggesting that I might want to visit the orphanage with him one day, or if not, perhaps make a donation . . . No? Well I'm sure you have your own charities, what am I thinking! By the end I felt like I had just sat through a brilliant one-man show, well worth the five dollars for me, and I had to assume, as inconse-quential as my contribution to the cause had been, that it had been worth his time too. I hopped into a tuk-tuk completely satisfied.

When I returned to my hotel, I unwrapped the vial, and it had been switched out. Instead of the clear lotus oil, the oil was brown. I opened it, and it smelled like very old frying oil.

My admiration was complete.

THE HIGHER EDUCATION IN TAMIL NADU

Kumbakonam, India

Several guides offered their services as I approached the Ramaswamy Temple in Kumbakonam, in the middle of Tamil Nadu. I said no thank you to each and smiled and passed on to the entrance.

Please, one said, following me, I am a student, and to pay for my studies I work as a guide to this temple. I can give very good service and you can help me to pay for my studies.

Where are you a student? I asked, turning and stopping. Moving forward and chatting would feel like a tacit acceptance of his services as guide, and I wasn't in the mood.

At the university here. There are very many interesting facts about this temple.

What do you study?

I am performing a BA in economics, he said. Also, I can tell you the significance of the different images, I can explain.

So are you taking classes now?

Yes, shall we go inside?

I'm sorry, which university?

Right here, he said, tossing a thumb over his shoulder. This is one of the most important temples in Tamil Nadu, originally built—

What classes are you taking, then, this semester?

This semester? Physics, he said.

Physics? And how many classes do you take altogether?

Right now I take seven, he said. I cannot take more because I need to work with the tourists to pay for my school.

And the seven classes, they are in physics?

Yes, mostly. Now.

That seems odd for an economics degree, I said. Seems like a lot of physics. What kind of physics?

All kinds! he said. You see it is a different kind of program here in India.

A physics-heavy economics BA, I said. Very interesting.

Yes, it is very interesting, exactly, it is university, very interesting. Shall we go in? I can explain the images.

Happy families wandered the temple grounds, with fresh daubs of color on their foreheads. I stopped to chat. My guide lost interest and wandered away. Very poor people, many old and disabled in one way or another, asked for money. I decided they needed my help more than the entrepreneur, anyway.

MY LIFE AS A PEDOPHILE
Malappuram, India

Driving at night is murderous in southern India, since all the same obstacles are on the road as in the day, but you can't see them. Overloaded hay wagons, children playing, men gossiping with a hand on a hip, endless dogs, beat-up reckless tuk-tuks, women with laundry, skeletal cows, bicycles, kids running in circles, furtive monkeys, the occasional elephant, farting cycles and scooters, oxcarts. Even the heavily decorated, barreling, careening, smoke-spewing trucks and buses often travel without lights. When dusk descends, you have to stop. Daylight trip times are unpredictable, depending on whether the road is just bad or miserable, and so I never knew where I would need to find a bed at the end of any given day.

One night, I ended up at dusk in the hills near the border of Tamil Nadu and Kerala and pulled into what was basically a truck stop, not a real town. I rented the best available room for two dollars, and I assume that was a gouge-the-tourist price. The bed was a hard mattress on the floor with bedding that may have been cleaned a week or two earlier, maybe not. I slept in my clothes and wrapped a T-shirt over my head. A demure prostitute knocked on the door to offer her services and was gracious when I declined. She was about fifty, weighed more than me, and her clothes were perhaps cleaner than the rags on my bed. She was very polite, sweet, and she smiled and bowed as she backed away, and I bowed and smiled, too, both us saying, *no hard feelings.*

I got back on the road in the morning unscathed, no bugs, no bites, and drove all day. Along the highway a holy man had built a tiny chapel, and I stopped and poked my head in. Arms stretched I could touch both side walls, and it was less than twice that in length. The holy man had a concave chest, wore a loin cloth and nothing else, had gray hair and an intermittent gray beard, and his face had a series of brightly colored smudges and swooshes. Each meant something specific, although I didn't know the code. He was very happy to see me, encouraged me to come in, laughing at the pleasure of my visit, and invited me to look at his various altars. In the front he had a riot of stuff, like a badly curated Cornell box, or like a genius one: traditional figurines, scraps of commercial signage, calendars from petrol companies, pieces of colored glass, engine parts, contraptions for burning incense, empty soda cans, a hair comb, a very old tennis ball, framed pictures of people in Western clothes, plastic-framed mirrors, all of it a bit dusty. He posed for a few pictures and anointed my forehead with some chalky powder from a series of brightly colored piles. We spent some time communing, interrupted as several people ducked their heads in, most of whom seemed to be regulars. He would put a smear of color on their foreheads, and they would put a small coin on his tray. Even though I can often feel as if I've really communicated with someone, even with no language in common, in this case I was somewhat at a loss. I had no idea whether he wanted me to understand anything about his temple, his altar, his thoughts. All I could see was that he was infectiously happy, a true holy fool. I put a couple coins on his tray as I was leaving, and he gave me a big, chuckling, happy hug goodbye. It was truly warm, happily compassionate. If I lived there I would stop in every day, too.

That night, I pulled into a town, Malappuram, I knew nothing about, again needing to stop at dusk and get a room. I checked in and went for a stroll, looking for a place to eat, and in an open square in the center of town, as the light was fading, a lad, maybe fourteen, came up on a bicycle and said hello. He was a sweet kid, with a kindly face and bright eyes. He had fairly good English and asked me if I needed anything, and I said I was looking for a restaurant. He pointed up past my hotel; I'd walked in the wrong direction. He kept finding new things to talk about, but I was getting hungry, and after a while I just said okay, time for me to go to dinner. He rode away, and immediately another kid, this one around twelve, came up on a bike and rode alongside me and talked for a while, following me as I headed toward the restaurants. I assumed they would ask for money, but they never did.

I had my dinner, went back to my room, and read up on the town I was in. It turns out that it is a sex tourism location for European men looking for young Indian boys. The next morning as I went down to breakfast, I saw other Western men, by themselves, in the hotel dining room. They all looked a little uncomfortable. And I started playing back all the scenes of the day before. The looks I got from the people at the hotel desk, the people at the restaurant, people on the street, the kids on their bikes of course. Every one of them had assumed I was a sex tourist there for the boys. I felt vaguely ashamed. I noticed that as I checked out and got in my car, my head was bowed, as if I was trying to hide, much like the guys at breakfast. I was, for that day, in the eyes of the world, a pedophile sex tourist. It is not a pleasant way to walk around.

Do they, I wondered, feel that they are invisible? I saw a man, as I was about to drive off, who looked German, maybe sixty years old, very white, overweight. He glanced up and saw me looking at him. He furtively turned, hunching away from my gaze. He clearly didn't feel invisible when he saw me, but maybe the rest of the time he felt just as I do, mostly, when I travel, that nobody recognizes the real me, that I am safely anonymous. That feeling—the liberating sense that nobody knows who I am, that I am a cipher—I had always found one of the pleasures of travel. I was going to have to rethink that.

MIDDLE EAST
AND
CENTRAL ASIA

THE LITTLE MAN OF SAMARKAND
Samarkand, Uzbekistan

At the market in Samarkand—the size of an airport terminal, with
endless tables of produce, meat, nuts, grains, spices, fish, and dried
fruit—this little kid, in a neat and pressed though slightly stained
and frayed school uniform of white shirt and navy slacks, maybe
twelve years old, came up to me and asked me whether I spoke
English, and if he could practice his English with me. I said, fine,
sure. He attached himself to me for the next five hours and basically
never stopped talking, until the last hour that is. Preternaturally
mature, and unintentionally funny as a result, he had become a
minor celebrity in the market, with all the older people watching in
amazement as this precocious and unself-conscious kid spoke fluent
English to me, like the young Jesus talking to the rabbis.

Not a lot of English is spoken in Samarkand, and certainly not in
the wholesale market. A very upright, sweet, innocent, earnest prod-
igy, the kid immediately engaged me in a conversation about who
I was, where I was from, what I had done so far in Uzbekistan, and
what I hoped to do. Along the way he told me a few things about himself, such as how old he was, how many brothers and sisters, where
he learned English—but he was his least favorite subject through
much of the day. Many people already knew him and asked him questions as we walked by, and he then translated the questions for me
and translated my answers. Every day, he said, he went to the American embassy, where he got free pens and free use of the library. He

was also a student at a local language school—a pretty good school, he thought, though he knew he didn't really know since he had not been to other language schools, so he couldn't compare them, but he knew that it was much, much better than his regular school, which he knew was very bad, and he felt that his English had improved considerably—did I think his English was improving? Well, not improving, because I wouldn't be able to tell that, since we just met, but he wanted my honest appraisal of his English skills, he was quite determined to get to be a fluent speaker of English. What did I think?

And he was like that, always, a frank but polite and unaffected motormouth. As we walked through the market, he explained to me everything that caught my eye, and it seemed that each new vendor, every few feet, had something to say to him. You could see they were impressed. The kid was a natural, completely at home in his own skin, more like a shrunken adult than a boy. He would take out a small notebook and write down the words—usually the names of fruits or other foodstuffs—that he could not find the English word for, always keeping up his running commentary. A woman with a baby begged me for money. I gave her some and was swarmed by a bunch of other women with babies. He stood aside but shook his head.

Bad idea? I asked.

You should not give them money, he said. They have more money than you or me. And their husbands just lie around the house.

It pained him to report this, I could see. He was not at all dour but very serious, and he wanted to put as good a face on things as he could honestly manage. He asked what my plans were for the rest of the day. I told him I wanted to see a certain mosque.

We will need to take two busses, he said. Would you like to go now?

Yes, I said, I would.

I'm afraid I will not be able to accompany you, he said, because I do not have the bus fare, but I can take you to the bus stop and talk to the driver, so he helps you, so he can tell you what is the right stop, the stop where you will get the second bus. He looked a bit nervous, like he wasn't sure if I would be able to manage without his help.

Would you please act as my tour guide? I said. I am happy to pay your bus fare. I can hire you to be my guide.

He thought about this for a minute.

I do not think I have the proper knowledge of the mosque, he said, to be a very good guide. He thought some more. I do not believe I can be a very good guide. But I think I would like to be a guide, and I will work to learn more so that I can be a guide to more than the market. I think I am a very good guide to the market now, but I would like to be a good guide to the mosques and the tombs and the madrassas, also.

Well, this can be practice then, I said, and you can find out what you need to know.

For the first time he became the excited boy rather than the rational miniadult. I will tell my sister I am going on my first job as a guide! You wait here! Or—he stopped himself—I will tell her that I am training to be a guide. I will return very quickly!

He ran off into the crowd, and a few minutes later he was back with a girl a few years older.

My sister will tell my mother I am working as a guide and will come home soon, he said. She shrugged, like *big deal*.

We get the bus here, he said, walking toward the corner.

We got on a crowded city bus for a couple of miles. He was jabbering away about his family (I had asked), and the people around us, much like the bystanders in the market, were astounded by his fluency. We got off that bus and onto another, and he continued his gabbing, speculating on how he would learn what he needed to know. I suggested getting an English-language travel guidebook, which would give capsule histories and descriptions of each of the sights, which he could then augment with other material. He pulled out his notebook, wrote the word *augment* followed by *add to*, and was about launch into a new train of thought when he stopped short with a gasp.

What is it? I asked.

That man, he said, quietly.

He poked a girl next to him and glanced from her purse to the man standing on the other side of her. She checked her purse and yelled and grabbed the man's arm, but he wrestled free and tried to get off the bus, which was stopping. The kid who collected fares grabbed him, the guy dropped the phone he had lifted from the girl's purse, and people began shouting. The thief, who was in his forties and harried and nasty looking, pointed at the phone, now on the floor of the bus, apparently claiming the girl had just dropped it—she bent down and angrily picked it up, spitting mad and yelling at him—and then the thief wrestled away from the ticket taker and took off running, pursued by his captor and another passenger. The bus driver, who had pulled the emergency brake, had jumped down and was now in hot pursuit too. We all sat or stood on the bus and watched them chase the man across the highway and into a field. They disappeared behind some buildings, and the kid said he had seen the man take her phone.

But, oh, no, he said, deeply plaintive, and he was very agitated, swaying back and forth and wringing his hands. This is bad.

The men from the bus reappeared, dragging the thief back by the shirt and arms, the bus driver talking on his cell phone, calling the police, I assumed.

When they pushed the man back onto the bus, it sent my kid into a panic, and he ducked down between my shins and the seatback in front of me, cowering, like Pip hiding from Magwitch, claiming, in a panicked whisper, that the thief had seen him warn the girl and now would kill him. At the next stop, he literally crawled out through the thirty people in the aisle, me following upright, to slip out the back door.

He then never stopped talking about how afraid he was, slapping his notebook into his other hand, berating himself for getting involved.

But how would that man ever find you? I asked. Do you know him?

No, he said, but I am well known now because of my English, and so many people know me now, and that man looked right at me, and I could tell he meant to find me and kill me.

I don't think—I started to say that it seemed implausible, but what did I know?

He had not forgotten his original mission, and we had left the bus at the correct stop for the mosque. He motioned me to follow across the street and a large square to the enormous, well-appointed mosque, where he approached an old, white-bearded imam and explained the whole situation to him. The imam listened attentively, and then they bowed their heads. The imam said a prayer, silently, eyes closed, standing with a hand on the boy's shoulder. When he was done, he looked the kid in the eye and talked to him, very seriously. Then he went on his way.

The kid was still disconsolate. Apologizing to me, he sat on the mosque's steps and held his little overstuffed head in his hands and stayed perfectly still, miserable.

What did the imam say? I asked.

I asked him, how do you say *ask the god*?

Pray?

Yes, pray—I know that already, but I am upset—I asked him to pray for me for God to not let that man kill me.

And what did he say to that?

That Allah knows I did the right thing, and Allah will protect me.

But that doesn't make you feel better?

No.

He will probably go to jail, the thief, I said.

He has friends.

You know this? His head was still in his hands, he was despondent.

No. He paused for a moment and then said, I worry for my family.

Won't he be mad at the bus driver, the ticket taker, the other man who chased him down? They are the ones who gave him to the police. Will he kill everyone? The girl too?

I was the one who made him trouble, the boy said. He looked right at me, he knew I was the one.

On the way back, on the second bus, he was not his talkative self. When we arrived back where we started, I gave him five dollars and told him not to worry. He could not shake it, though, and remained subdued.

This is a very generous payment, and I appreciate it very much, he said. I have to go home now.

And without any more ceremony he turned to go. Then he stopped and turned back toward me.

I will be free tomorrow, he said quietly. You can look for me here at the market.

ARMENIA IS NOT BEAUTIFUL
Baku, Azerbaijan

Where are you going? asked the pleasant young woman at the rental car counter.

I thought I would go to Quba, I said.

Beautiful.

And maybe Sheki.

Ah, that is very beautiful.

And then into Georgia.

Ah, Georgia is also beautiful. She looked at me, handing me my papers.

But not Armenia, she volunteered.

No?

She was about twenty-five and had the thick, raven hair of most Azeri women and a very winning smile.

No, Armenia is not beautiful.

No?

No, not beautiful, not beautiful. She shook her head. The Armenians and Azeris have a long history of conflict and have been at war, this time, since 1988, when the region known as Nagorno-Karabakh, then largely and now entirely settled by ethnic Armenians, voted to secede from Azerbaijan and become part of Armenia. There has been an official cease-fire since 1994, but there are still dozens of clashes each year, and nobody of Armenian descent is allowed entry into

Azerbaijan. Nagorno-Karabakh, almost surrounded by Azerbaijan, has proclaimed itself an independent nation, and is accessible only through Armenia.

I can take this car into Georgia?

Yes, she said. No problem. But you will buy new insurance at the border. Very simple.

And I can take the car to Armenia?

No, she said. That is impossible.

I caught her eyes. They flashed full of hate, but just for a moment.

Do you want the GPS? she asked, smiling once more.

AT THE BORDER
Lagodekhi, Georgia–Balakan, Azerbaijan

Can I go to Georgia, I asked at the Azerbaijan border station, and come back?

Of course! The official said. Two of them were in the booth, and the first one I talked to didn't have any English. Nonetheless, he stood to the side and nodded reassuringly.

No problem getting back in? I asked.

No problem, he said. The other nodded again. They both were around thirty-five, and this was a low-pressure job. There was very little traffic in either direction—very few people, in fact. Mountains rose to the north above semiarid pine forest, some dusty farm fields, and the occasional house. I had a sense that these were men who were fine with their station in life, though, and with the quietness. The English speaker was a bit lighter skinned, a bit more languid, maybe not as quick, mentally as his darker coworker. The coworker had a two o'clock shadow.

I can take the car into Georgia?

Yes. You buy insurance. Across border.

And I can bring it back?

Of course!

I had come from Sheki, with its elaborate eighteenth-century palace and caravanserai, one of the major Silk Road towns. It had once seen traffic from Tehran, Baghdad, Tashkent, Istanbul, Damascus, Cairo, and Kashgar, much more traffic than it gets today. Nowadays, most of the visitors are Azeris from Baku—it is a popular destination. The road toward Georgia ran northwest alongside the mountains— the Caucasus Mountains that form both countries' northern border with Russia—and I had been driving it some four or five hours, stopping at Sheki and Zaqatala, trying a few side roads up into the mountains. For many of those miles, there had been nothing but forest.

I have a single entry visa, I said.

Yes, he said. The darker man nodded.

But I can come back?

Yes, of course!

But I have to get another visa?

Yes, no problem.

I cannot use this visa?

No. Single entry means one entry. You are here.

Can I get a new visa here at the border when I come back in a few days?

No.

Where, then?

I don't know. From ministry.

Is there an embassy in Tbilisi?

Of course.

And I can get a visa there.

Yes.

I was beginning to get a sense that *yes* was different than *of course*. Maybe yes was halfway between *of course* and *I don't know*; but maybe it was halfway between *of course* and *no*.

Yes? Or maybe?

Yes.

How long will it take?

Some weeks.

Ah! I said. I don't have some weeks to stay in Georgia.

He shrugged. He really didn't care whether I went to Tbilisi, or if I came back.

I have a ticket from Baku to Tehran in four days. I just wanted run up and see the capital and come back, two days.

He shrugged again.

Many Azeris in Iran, he said.

Yes, I said. In the north.

Other place too, he said, Tehran, Isfahan.

The police were thoroughly corrupt in Azerbaijan, which I had learned the hard way, paying hundreds of euros in fines for invented infractions. I had finally learned how to bargain and now only paid five euros when I was stopped. At first they were getting more than a hundred from me.

I wondered if the border guards were similarly bribable.

Is it possible, I asked, to give gifts to border guards?

Of course, he said, and smiled. The other nodded and also smiled. They didn't know where this was going, but how could it be bad?

Is there a gift that would allow a second entry on a single-entry visa?

Oh, he said, it is possible.

The other guard was shaking his head no. They had a little confab.

It is not possible, he said.

Are you sure?

We have to record that you leave Azerbaijan.

Why? I asked. Who will know?

You maybe come back, you maybe don't come back.

I have a rental car from Baku. I have to come back.

He shrugged.

Car is stolen, he said. You are dead. This is bad for us.

The one who didn't speak English laughed.

Yes, I said. Bad for me too!

They laughed politely.

Can I get a new visa in Tbilisi in one day? Also with a gift?

They had another little confab.

Not possible. Visa has to go to Baku and come back. Some days, maybe, with money.

I cannot go to Georgia, I said.

Yes, he said. His partner nodded.

Georgia is beautiful? I asked.

He pointed to the mountain behind me and said Azerbaijan, then pointed to mountain a mile away to the north and said Georgia. Then he pointed to the first mountain.

This is beautiful? he asked.

I shrugged. It was nice to have a turn. Of course, I said.

Then you think Georgia beautiful, he said. They smiled.

But they were getting bored. The darker one picked up a newspaper.

Okay, thanks, *tesikkur edirem*, I said.

He gave me a small ironic salute and closed his window.

I drove back south.

WINDCATCHERS
Yazd, Iran

Iran is a big country, and its major cities all very different. Yazd is the desert city, some four hundred miles south of Tehran, and the old parts of town look like many Silk Road cities—stone domes the color of the surrounding sand—but in this case studded with square towers, sticking up like oversized chimneys on almost every building. Even medium-sized houses sometimes had more than one.

They are *bâdgir*s, or windcatchers, part of a millennia-old system of cooling. The most basic simply have an open face that catches the prevailing wind, which then gets pushed down into the house, eventually rising and exiting the other side, acting like a big fan to move air. Other systems are more elaborate and send air down into an underground *qanat*, or canal, which cools the air; it then rises into the house, where it eventually heats back up, rises again, and exits from a second tower.

The results are so effective that in the middle of the day, which in the summer is always 100 to 110 degrees Fahrenheit, nobody is on the street except me, a lone American wandering around, sun-dazed.

The combination of inhospitable climate and air-conditioning meant that people stayed home and had forgotten how to be friendly. The few people I found looked at me suspiciously.

Just south of town is a famous Zoroastrian site where the bodies of the dead were left on round towers for the buzzards to eat. There was nobody there, either.

GRIEVING WITH THE POETS

Takht-e Jamshid–Shiraz, Iran

The Greeks called it Persepolis, the city of the Persians, but the Iranians call it Takht-e Jamshid, the throne of Jamshid, the mythical first king of Persia. Burned by Alexander in 330 BCE, it never came back. The ruins of the great palaces and gates built by Darius the Great in the sixth century BCE have the grandeur of the Parthenon on the Acropolis, but the relief work and the statuary have a flavor more Egyptian than Greek, the human and animal figures stylized rather than realist. It is one of the most impressive archaeological sites in the world, and the main reason foreign tourists go to Shiraz.

The main reason Iranians go to Shiraz, though, is to visit the tomb of fourteenth-century poet Hafez, the most popular poet in Persian history. The marble tomb sits under an open pavilion, a kind of ornate gazebo, in the Musalla Gardens on the northeast edge of the city, near the Qur'an Gate. At the entrance to the gardens men have small birds, budgies or finches, who will pick a verse of Hafez's poetry from a small box with their beaks and drop it in your palm. Fortune-tellers elsewhere in Iran use birds in this way and use other quotations and verses alongside those of Hafez, and the randomness of the method (or the magical intuition of the birds) seems to be the draw, since so many people, especially those visiting the tomb, have committed many verses to memory already. The pilgrims to the site walk to the tomb, lay a hand on the marble cover of the sarcophagus, and recite the verses to themselves, aloud or silently. Many stay for a while, engrossed in meditation or prayer, almost always in a state of ecstatic distress. Many weep. All ages, men and women, all walks of life participate, and these acts of literary engulfment are not occasions for shame or pride. They remain, however public the place, private moments.

Hafez's poetry, some of it love poetry, some paeans to drink, some devotional, is full of complex, intense emotions, and Iranians are intensely devoted to the poetic word, to lyric. The two things people agreed on, wherever I went, were the importance of engineering and the importance of poetry. People gather every night to sing traditional lyric poetry, with the verses of many traditional songs drawn from the poetry of Hafez, and Hafez Day is a national holiday.

I started asking people to recite their favorite Hafez poem for me, and everyone I asked had at least a couplet at the ready; they were in Farsi, of course, and so I couldn't understand them, but the emotional tenor of them was hard to miss. A young man in Isfahan, studying to be an engineer, a buttoned up, unassuming, conservative kid, when I asked whether he knew any verses, went on for a few minutes, and by the time he was done he had tears on his cheeks. He apologized, but only pro forma, the way he apologized for his accent, which was not bad at all—he said he was sorry in a way that made it clear that he was quite proud of his performance, and it had quite clearly reinvigorated him.

At the tomb of Hafez too, people were fortified by their visits. I watched an older woman for some ten minutes as she communed with the spirit of the long-dead poet. She arose, and walked away, eyes red and wet, bolstered, full of breath, triumphant.

PARADISE
Dubai, United Arab Emirates

Many countries try to restrict internet access, but I have found—in Iran, in China—that even the simplest proxy server arrangements will let you get wherever you want to go. That is, if the web is working at all, if they don't turn it off completely. The Emirates, though, have an enormous amount of money, and they know how to shut down just what they want to shut down.

Eighty percent of the population is in the servant and worker class, all of whom are immigrants or temporary workers. Human Rights Watch calls their treatment "less than humane"; others call it slavery. Seventeen percent of the population is Emirati. Oil-swollen government coffers mean that they have the wherewithal to hire as many IT people as required to keep the flow of information perfectly modulated. Not only did my proxies not work, the pages that discussed how to set up proxies were blocked. The pages that discussed censoring the internet were blocked. Somewhere, a huge staff was kept busy making sure that the Arab Spring never arrived. I could not access my own site to update it.

Throughout Dubai, from the airport to the hotels to the shopping centers, one finds foreigners doing all and any actual labor, and locals in the whitest of white linens overseeing it. The blindingly white robe is an interesting choice. White clothing has also been worn by certain Southern gentlemen (Samuel Clemens, Tom Wolfe, Boss Hawg, plantation owners) and by certain clerics, imams, and

Catholic priests, and whatever else it might signal, it is a color that says you are not working—certainly not doing anything where any part of you might get dirty. White clothes—as in the case of tennis or yachting duds—announce your leisure status, that you are beyond all drudgery, that you do not need to lift a finger.

The same white-robed men, and their wives in the most sumptuous of black niqabs and Gucci sunglasses, live in a world apart. The men may nominally be executives of some sort, but they are never seen working, these men all in white. The women shop while being trailed by Pakistani and Indian manservants pushing handcarts full of packages and designer-store shopping bags, their children trailed, one on one, by nannies. The American South in 1850 is the most obvious parallel—tasks separated by races, the dominant race absolutely unconcerned about how they might appear to an outside gaze, comfortable in their racial superiority, at home in what they assume to be their God-given splendor. Both genders, in the ruling class, flash bling from beneath their voluminous drapes. The servants walk an appropriate number of steps behind.

In the shops and behind hotel desks, immigrants from Syria and other Arab countries function as a tiny middle class. I asked a man running a clothing store, in the one part of town that had not been replaced by malls, what it was like to be an immigrant in Dubai, to not be an Emirati.

It is better than being where I come from, of course, he said, smiling. Why else would we all come?

Are you second-class citizens?

No, he said, we are not citizens, he said, we are guest workers.

So you don't own this shop?

He laughed, and said, no, not possible, I am not Emirati.

And will you go back to Syria?

Perhaps, he said, when I retire.

He was about forty.

That is many years, I said.

I make a living, he said, one eyebrow raised. Is this not enough?

CROSSING THE BORDER
Eilat, Israel

My first attempt to cross the border into Israel from the Sinai Peninsula was rebuffed. I had ended up wandering in the hills in my rental car as the sun was setting, and my map showed a crossing. As I approached, several Israeli soldiers were watching over an immigration official as he checked the passports of a line of poor Arabs on their way in. The petitioners wore dusty peasant garb. They were lined up against a chain-link fence. There were no other cars, only a solitary Israeli army jeep on the other side of the fence, and I realized that the only passage through the fence was a three-foot door. There was no vehicle-sized gate. I got out of my car and approached, but the soldiers waved me away. It was clear to them, long before it was clear to me, that this checkpoint was not for me, not for anyone like me. This was not even, I sensed, for people going to Eilat, Israel's southernmost city only a dozen miles away, but for country people chasing their sheep, tending fields, working the grudging land.

When I got to the main border crossing, I had to leave my car in a parking lot, walk across, and take a cab to the nearest rental car office. In the age of car bombs, Egyptian cars were not welcome in Israel.

Coming into Israel after time in Egypt, one is immediately struck by the money, by the wealth, as when returning to the United States from Mexico. Substandard infrastructure is replaced by the latest innovations, unlighted two-lane macadam is replaced by a floodlit divided multilane highway, and the waiting cabs were all late-model Mercedes sedans. Small wonder, I thought, anti-Semitism aside, resentment abounds.

I got in a leather-upholstered Mercedes and was whisked into the city of Eilat, where I didn't have to bargain with the Avis Rent-a-Car clerk to get the price I got online, and everyone at restaurants, hotels, and gas stations took credit cards rather than insisting on cash. Cafés and shops were up to date and sparkling. The line of dusty shepherds waiting to enter Israel through the chain-link fence seemed a world away. Islam and Judaism seemed unimportant compared to the half century or century that seemed to separate the two cultures and the palpable, immense difference in GDP.

But of course, this is just projection on my part. A man in a shop in Cairo, talking about a bombing that had occurred the week before in Jerusalem, said, it is terrible, yes, I hate to see any loss of life, anyone get hurt. But for the Jews, he said, this is good. They need to understand they don't belong here. They need to go. I asked him if he had ever been to Israel, and he laughed and said no. I asked him if he had ever met a Jew, and he said he thought so.

EVERYONE BELONGS SOMEWHERE

Gold Souk, Amman, Jordan

Al Quds Restaurant, they said, right around the corner. I had asked a couple of guys hanging out in front of their luggage shop where to eat.

I can't figure out how these tiny shops in cities like Amman survive. I counted five used watch shops on my way from the parking structure—actually in the hallway of the parking structure—and an empty stall was being refitted for a sixth. Not a single one had a customer. The three workers and the owner and someone else were all in the new shop, discussing glass shelving, and I thought, how will they ever pay for what they are doing today, much less support this guy's family? How will he ever sell enough used watches, with all this competition, in this dingy hallway?

I had a nice chat with the luggage guys for fifteen minutes or so, during which no customer stopped in. They didn't seem concerned. In the Mango Souk, the cloth and clothing market, bolts and bolts of shiny, bright cloth stretched from the street to deep interiors, the bolts looking like fresh jumbo boxes of Crayolas. The shopkeepers made a half-hearted attempt to entice a few bored women walking by to look at their wares. They rarely succeeded. One shop had two window displays, each with four mannequins, all wearing Fredericks of Hollywood trashy lingerie—one Superwoman themed, one Batgirl, a policewoman's uniform, a few lazy versions of the teddy, one with crotchless frilled panties. All made with less fabric than a single headscarf. More than half the women walking by were in hijab. Nobody came in to that store or out. Nobody seemed to be actually shopping.

The restaurant, however, Al Quds—the Arab name for Jerusalem—was booming. The front of the shop is taken up by a baklava counter, with meter-circumference pans of a half-dozen different varieties, most sprinkled with green chips of pistachio, as impressive a desert display as I've ever seen, and I've been to the Carnegie Deli. And like the Carnegie Deli, there's nothing fancy about the decor, no attempt to wow with furniture, wall treatments, place settings. Instead of napkins there's a box of coarse tissue in the center of the table. Of course, unlike the Carnegie Deli, here there are zero Jews. There are, however, all the varieties of dress, women wearing the full niqab to just the standard scarf to, in one case, no scarf at all. But most common is what I came to think of as the Jordanian scarf, which is very glamorous, colorful, and very large, I assume because there is an enormous hairdo underneath, the kind of huge, elegant bun sticking backward on the same angle as Nefertiti's headdress—the effect is more like Sophia Loren in the 1960s than the conservative headgear of the countryside.

Two-thirds of the men were in Western dress, the other third in the three different versions of djellaba—the white, tailored, Emirate high-style, with a Nehru collar and a lot of starch, form fitting and blindingly white; the somewhat more relaxed whites, browns, and grays of ordinary men; and the dumpy, coarse-fibered loose-fitting old man's getup. I got the sense that the higher the style, the more of a statement was being made—the old men were dressing just as they had in their villages a half century ago and didn't think much of it. The guys with the Gucci glasses, ostentatious watches, and gold pens in their front pockets were saying either *we will bury you* to the West or *I will bury you* to their business competitors or *I don't care if I bury you or not, I have much more money than you* to everyone. The headgear signified, too—the most striking the Syrian red-and-white keffiyeh, either wrapped or held on with an *ogal* made of black braided rope. Others wore an assortment of knit skullcaps, some looking African, some Central Asian, making quieter statements.

The waiters, like waiters in any service-heavy restaurant, had a hierarchy: the older guys in a suit and tie or suit and bow tie, with deep, almost scary authority; their assistants, in black vests and bow ties; then the busboys and assistants in a kind of tunic. These last never interacted directly with the customers. The headwaiter took the order and handed it to an assistant. The assistant looked at it and handed it to the factotum, who took it into the kitchen. The factotum brought the food out from the kitchen on a tray, and for low-class diners, the assistant checked the tray, then gave the nod to have it delivered to the table. Middle-class customers got the assistant's delivery. The headwaiters almost never touch food, except in the case of very important customers; then they come in and swan a dish or two in front of the sheik or the imam or the captain of industry. When big wheels come in, they get a bow from the haughty headwaiters, who make a great show of choosing a table and generally fuss over them. They never stop scanning the important tables.

One of the waiters, standing two feet from an underling, waved him over impatiently. It would have taken less effort to make the one step toward him. The underlings bow their heads, always, in front of their superiors and shuffle-hustle away on errands. One young middle-rank guy, I noticed, was especially curt with his helpers. He was on his way to the top rank, you could see it—he assumed authority, he reveled in it, he wore it like armor.

On the way out of Jordan that night, in the airport, I got into a conversation with a guy who was about to retire from the U.S. Army. He had just been assigned as a consultant for the last few months to the Jordanian army, where he was doing some training, he told me, though he avoided being specific about it. He had been stationed many different places around the Middle East and around the world; this was just his latest posting.

I asked him if he had noticed the intense hierarchies in everyday life in Jordan, for instance, among the waiters at Al Quds. He seemed to think it was true in most places.

Except in America, he said. We pretend there is no hierarchy. In the army, of course, hierarchy comes with the territory.

We had a drink, and I asked him whether people at his level in the service ever doubted the mission.

Of course, he said. Or, more often, we doubt *a* mission. We talk about it—like, that was stupid, or that's a bad, bad decision. But I didn't ever *want* to be at that level where you *make* decisions. I leave that to the folks who want it. That's your hierarchy right there. You want the big suit? You gotta deal with it.

I asked him what he was going to do when he retired. He was in his early forties. He said he would undoubtedly work for a military contractor.

A bunch of them have already been in touch, he said.

So they want you to work for them doing the kind of training you're doing now?

He laughed.

No, they don't care what I know, he said. They want me, really, for just two things: they want my security clearance—it would cost them a hundred grand to move somebody new through that mess of paperwork; and they want my Rolodex—who do we talk to to sell this thing? Who do we talk to to sell that? It's business. They want more contracts. That's what they do. They don't do war, they don't do peace, they do contracts. They're contractors!

So it doesn't matter that you know Jordan?

Not really. These guys who are talking to me, they have business everywhere. If this shop closes down, another will open up. There are always new customers.

He caught his plane, and I chatted with a Palestinian woman who lived in Jordan and whose kid was running wild.

Your English has no accent, I said.

Yeah, most of my life I lived in Michigan. My father was a graduate student at CalTech and then a professor at Michigan. We're going to Michigan now.

Her kid had wandered off and was running a luggage cart across the room. She excused herself and ran him down.

And your flight comes through Amman? I asked when she got back.

She looked at me, quizzical.

No, we live in Jordan.

Oh, I thought you said Palestinian.

Like most Palestinians, she said, I never lived in Palestine. Excuse me.

She got up to chase after the kid again. She seemed to have no parenting technique beyond running after him, picking him up, and putting him back down closer to where she was.

Your husband is Jordanian?

No, he is Palestinian too. We met when we were both graduate students at University of Pennsylvania. He also taught at MIT. But now he has a company, and so we've been in Jordan for two years now.

And then you go back to the States?

No, the company is here, we are here. The kid was banging one of her suitcases into a wall. She started to get up to stop him and changed her mind, sat back down. He continued banging.

She asked about my travels in Jordan, and I told her a couple stories, and then about the Jordanian kid I talked to on the Petra highway, who told me Americans invaded Iraq because they hate Muslims.

She shrugged, made that slight clown frown that means *what else do you expect?*

You think so too? I asked.

America kills many people, she said. Have you noticed they are all Muslims?

Her kid came over and demanded a drink. He was the boss, she the factotum.

Excuse me, she said, and got up to follow him as he ran toward the kiosk.

BAD NEIGHBORHOOD
Izmir, Turkey

The rug salesmen, all across the Maghreb, from Morocco back
around to Turkey, have very similar sales techniques; they vary only
in intensity. In Izmir, the bazaar where I found myself had a very
relaxed group, and we had our obligatory cup of tea, and when it
became clear I wasn't going to buy a rug, we started to have a chat.

We sat and talked about the things I had seen—the Hittite ruins at
Boğazkale, the underground carved-rock churches in Cappadocia,
the wonders of Istanbul—and we talked about Turkey's special place
in the world, its historic function as the crossroads of East and West,
and, gingerly, the Kurdish rebellion.

You have to imagine, one man said, how embattled it feels to be
Turkey. He was about forty-five, a solid-citizen type.

Yes! another said, older, smoking. Can you imagine having such
neighbors? he said, waving his arms. Iraq! Iran! Syria! Armenia!
Greece! These are horrid people!

(I took a ferry, shortly after this, to Lesbos, the Greek island closest
to Turkey, and while I was there, a woman in her eighties who had
been a cultural attaché, the daughter of a famous novelist, glanced
over her shoulder at the nearby Turkish coast and literally shud-
dered. Even after all these years, she said, I cannot think of that place
without horror.)

We are, the first man said, very cosmopolitan. But it is difficult.

We had a long discussion of American foreign policy. Nobody was happy about it. Everyone commiserated, though, granting the difficulties of being in the crosshairs of so many different competing interests. This was before Syria boiled over, and the Kurds were still considered Turkey's biggest problem. The Kurdish rebellion was clearly a hot topic, and they sensed I might not agree with them, so they glossed over it.

The U.S. is very much like Turkey, the older man said, and everyone nodded in approval, as a boy poured more tea.

Eventually I bought a rug, a big rug, and schlepped it home.

THE AMERICAS

SEMANA SANTA

Tecún Umán –San Juan Ostuncalco-Antigua, Guatemala

Tourists do not drive to Tecún Umán. One of the secondary border
crossings from Guatemala into Mexico, it is about forty miles up
from the Pacific coast and 150 miles northwest of the capital. I was
running late—as I approached the town, the sun was setting, and I
had been warned against driving at night. In fact, most guidebooks
and the U.S. State Department advised against leaving your hotel at
night. A mile or two short of town, a flash of movement caught my
eye, in the bushes, and I thought I saw a group of young men with
bandanas over their faces, wearing sunglasses in the gloomy dusk,
knit caps, and what looked like oversized clothes and fatigues. And
carrying rifles.

Guerrillas!

My god! The revolution was breaking out right in front of me. I
slowed to a stop and turned around in my seat to see what was happening. They had crossed the road and were going into the one open
business on that stretch—it looked like a shop and bar with some
tables out front. I rolled down my window and heard music and the
sound of laughter. I pulled the car around and headed back, and as
I got closer I saw that one of the masked men was carrying what
looked like a huge dummy, dressed exactly like himself, with a ban-
dana, sunglasses and everything, but several feet taller. Another, I
now saw, had a boom box. A third was clearly in drag. By the time

I got out of the car, they were dancing, the oversized dummy astride their shoulders, and I could see they were teenagers.

I had arrived in Guatemala during Holy Week. Each year, in the days before Good Friday, young men and boys dress up in scary costumes and demand change from everyone they come across: trick or treat. A few slightly drunk guys at the bar cheered these kids on and gave them some coins, after which they walked down the road to find more victims.

The next day, I wandered through many costumed groups, and among the goblins and ghouls were always a number of boys dressed as guerrillas—for them, it seems, just a costume, for me an anxious reminder of the long history of violence, revolution, repression, and invasion. It must have some such resonance for them as well.

The day I arrived in Guate, as the capital Guatemala City is called, the newspaper *Prensa Libre* had a front-page story about European governments naming the country one of the most dangerous places on earth. Murder rates are, in fact, among the highest in the world. Guards with automatic rifles stand outside hotels, at the entrance to parking lots, banks, shopping malls, and stores of any size. Police armed to the teeth operate roadblocks and roam the streets at all hours. Getting gas my first day, I noticed a man with a shotgun standing among the refueling cars and trucks. I thought it was a security guard for the gas station and was hoping he wouldn't shoot at anyone and blow up the gas station, but then he hopped into the cab of a meat truck as it drove away. He was quite literally riding shotgun on a load of cold cuts.

I checked into what everyone told me was the best hotel in Tecún Umán, and it was like an off-brand Nebraska motel away from the interstate. The town had that reek of desperation border towns often do. Poor people from Honduras and El Salvador think of Guatemala the way poor Mexicans think of the United States: a place, *con suerte*, to make some money, a dicey, dangerous, horrible promised land. And that's the way poor Guatemalans think of Mexico. Many were hanging around, waiting for a chance to slip into the place and find a better job. I had a piece of skirt steak and a beer for a bit under three dollars at a little place where the wood-fired grill, out on the sidewalk, was built out of half an oil drum. I gave out a few pesos to various hard cases that approached me in the very safe nighttime street—a man from El Salvador trying to get back into Mexico after being deported, a woman who was probably a speed freak, manic, addled, her face broken out.

Kids were out playing, teenagers zooming by on motorbikes. Lots of people, all ages, were interested in talking to the only tourist for miles. I said hello to the kids, took their pictures, showed them. The pretty girl with all the boys buzzing around her came over to see whether her magic worked on me too. I chatted in my mangled Spanish to the old men sitting in their plastic chairs, and they laughed at my mistakes. I had the pleasant feeling of being the gringo Roberto Benigni.

Life was difficult if you couldn't find work, they all agreed, and not everyone could find work. Many had relatives in Mexico City, in L.A., in San Diego. Some had spent time in Mexico themselves. It is hard, they said. They felt the weight of prosperous Mexico, big, exporting Mexico, sitting on their bent shoulders. Many Salvadorans and Hondurans think of the Guatemalans as stuck-up rich people with no hearts, and in Tecún Umán many felt that way about Mexicans. The dispossessed huddled at the borders, trying to find a way in, and this, they agreed, was inevitable when you have heartless people to the north. They glanced at me to see how I was taking that.

The next day, I wandered east through the coconut and banana groves along the border and then turned south into the mountains. In just a few miles I was in Mayan country. The air got cooler, the earth drier, the towns farther between, and life even closer to the bone. Very little traffic anywhere, and much of it animal-drawn— oxen and horses. In the mountains Spanish was most people's second language too, so I could converse better, all of us enunciating, speaking slowly. The hamlets were also slow, running at a rural rhythm, places where everyone knows the town drunk and women deliver bread on their heads. Between these tiny stucco towns, the men carried machetes and the women wore plain, floor-length Mayan skirts, and daily life remained, despite the TV antennas, largely unchanged year to year, the oxcarts still rolling on wooden wheels, firewood packed home on ponies.

In San Juan Ostuncalco I ran into my next bit of Semana Santa: a procession heading through the center of town, with a brass band playing a dirge for the death of Jesus, men in a variety of elaborate uniforms swinging incense censors, and thirty young Mayan women carrying on their shoulders a massive float in the shape of a gilded layer cake, a baroque casket, topped by life-sized statues of Christ lugging his cross and a half-dozen angels. The whole solemn march was flanked by hundreds of older Mayan women in bright woven skirts and headdresses. The cultural mix—European, Mayan, Catholic, pagan, ancient, medieval—was framed by the relentlessly contemporary: the musicians in their bebop shades and baseball caps, people on their cellphones as they walked, the traffic lined up and waiting to get through, the spaghetti of wires overhead.

I pressed on to one of Guatemala's main tourist attractions, Lago de Atitlán, a striking volcanic lake ringed with small, picturesque villages, all having their own celebrations, the streets full of sidewalk vendors and restaurants desperate for business, tchotchke shops, and overpriced hotels. The locals, as in any tourist town, are inured to strangers, sizing up prospects with a quick glance, deciding: mark or nuisance? The indigenous people in particular are sick of tourists taking their pictures.

Antigua Guatemala, fifty miles south across the mountains, people said, is where the very best Santa Semana experience was to be had, so I drove down. Antigua is a museum-quality site on every traveler's itinerary, a cobblestoned colonial town, rigorously maintained, extensively policed, full of history and surprisingly expensive second homes for the country's rich. On Good Friday and Holy Saturday processions originate every few hours from one of the six major churches in the city, each of them—with a large brass band and several hundred participants, carrying ridiculously oversized floats— wends its way through the city streets for hours. All day, one can hear, not too far away, the drumbeats that keep the purple- or black-robed *cucuruchos*, who carry the floats, walking in unison. They wear floor-length robes and tall peaked hats with masks, like Klansmen, or the Grim Reaper, giving the whole a sense of despair.

The streets are lined with thousands of onlookers, all eerily shrouded in smoke from hundreds of censors. The floats are the size of house trailers, lit up by gasoline-powered generators pulled by teams of young boys in the same robes. The forty-piece bands, hired for the occasion, are each church's major expense for the year. They are loud—almost entirely brass and drums—and they are funereal.

More impressive than the procession itself, though, are the *alfombras*—literally, carpets—made from pine needles, flowers, fruits, and colored sawdust, ten feet wide by as many as sixty feet long, laid down the center of the street. Families, neighbors, and friends labor over these intricate concoctions, spending many hours to reproduce images of Christ or the Virgin or geometric designs, outdoing their neighbors or their own efforts the previous year. I fell in with one family and helped a bit. The grandmothers sat in chairs and kibitzed, the young adults took charge, and the kids were sent on errands—more rose petals, more blue sawdust, more orange slices. I was befriended by a woman of sixty or so, Catherina, who looked like a nun, with short gray hair and a probing gaze. Many of the people working on the alfombra were her nieces and nephews, and grand-nieces and grandnephews. She had no children and had never married. Her father had been in the local government and had a written a history of the town, which she had studied. She knew everything, and didn't mind answering uninformed questions.

Like the Tibetan sand mandalas, the alfombras are destroyed as soon as they are finished, and work continued until the very last moment on ours—I felt some ownership, having been adopted as half mascot, half friend of the family's personage—right up until the minute the priests, the cucuruchos, and the bands arrived. The procession demolished the flowery carpet, of course, tromping across it and leaving it unrecognizable. Behind the last berobed marchers came men with shovels, brooms, and wheelbarrows, unceremoniously sweeping up the remains. Following them, a garbage truck, into which the wheelbarrows were emptied. The Buddhist sand paintings are swept away the minute they are completed; the alfombras are trampled as soon as they achieve their beauty and then dumped up into the garbage.

This always made sense to me as a Buddhist gesture, but it was an oddly counterintuitive image of the Easter message, a reminder not of rebirth, regeneration, and hope but of the fleetingness of life, a lesson in nonattachment, in disappearance, as if Christ had never been on the cross.

Antique Antigua, where a centuries-old four-bedroom house can cost a million and a half dollars, where the children of the rich come to party in their ancestral second homes, is an odd place or a lesson in the illusion of permanence. A *Prensa Libre* story the day before had warned that murders spike during Santa Semana, that Good Friday is the deadliest day of the year, but Antigua for all of Holy Week couldn't have been safer. Two policemen were stationed on every city block, around the clock. This zealous show of strength (and a heartless one—I talked to many policemen, shipped in from all over the country to keep Antigua safe for tourists and Antiguans, who were upset that they couldn't be with their own families during Santa Semana) served only to underline the great disparities of wealth, the poor sleeping on the streets of Tecún Umán while waiting to skip into Mexico, the rich celebrating ancient traditions in Antigua that are the stuff of violence.

They are also the stuff of migration, and one-fifth of all Guatemalans now live in Los Angeles. One-quarter of all Salvadorans too. Many of the Guatemalan Angelenos try to come back, if they can, to spend Santa Semana in the land of their birth.

The processions, whatever route they take, end, finally, in the main square in front of the cathedral. After our alfombra was swept away, I went with the family down to the square. Tens of thousands gathered to watch the processions make their circuit of the square.

Why, I asked Catherina, is it so moving?

Because, she said, it is so physical.

Do you see it is a bit ridiculous too? All this elaborate preparation for a parade, and just for an evening and it is over?

Yes, but all the preparation, all the labor, she said, is the point, as with the alfombras. And not just the preparation. Carrying the floats is very difficult—even strong men can only carry for twenty minutes at a time and then need to be replaced. The *andas* weigh two thousand, three thousand kilos, even four thousand. If just a few of the carriers fail, the float can crash, and if it does, people will be killed. It is very strenuous. And so the people feel, like Jesus did, the pain—Easter is rebirth, but Good Friday is about humiliation, torture, execution, death. It is very somber, and the arduous, backbreaking labor of carrying the anda is a reminder of the frailty of the body, and of suffering.

In the square, great floodlights pointed at the cathedral, others were aimed at the parade route, and the thick incense smoke everywhere made everything spectral. At different times more than one band was playing, and the cacophony, the tens of thousands of spectators, the statues of Christ carrying his cross and Mary weeping, lurching through the scene, and the crowd enraptured—the emotions were complicated, and no matter what Catherina said, I couldn't help thinking that the futility of the endeavor was part of the sense of tragedy that permeated the mood, however much buoyed by the aesthetic pleasures to be had. A brightly lit, small float went by, carried by eight sleepy boys, with a twice-life-sized skeleton holding a scythe in its left hand, its right hand lightly atop the arctic ice on a ten-foot globe. Death rules the world.

Given the intensity of this run-up, I expected Easter Sunday to be a wild celebration, but when I went out in the morning, the streets were empty. The celebration of death was, in fact, the end of the ritual. The cobblestones had a dusting of multicolored dyes, the only remnant of the night's extravagance.

LOS ANGELES, SOUTH
Nahuizalco, El Salvador

El Salvador had all the poverty and much less of the wealth of Guatemala. Shantytown villages lined the hillsides, and although San
Salvador was a hive of commercial activity, much of it was selling
bootlegged DVDs, odd-lot T-shirts offloaded by U.S. chains, and basic
household items. Much of the downtown commerce spreads out
into the street, business done in quasi-permanent stalls along the
sidewalks, spilling into the streets themselves—people selling used
machinery, used consumer items, used everything, like an open-air
flea market and dollar store. Tourist business when I was there in
the late 1990s was down to levels not seen since the 1960s due to the
double whammy of the lingering effects of the civil war of the 1980s
and the new threat posed by the repatriation of gang members from
La Mara Salvatrucha—the notorious gang of guys with tattooed faces
that formed in Los Angeles in the 1980s and began being deported in
droves after the passage of the 1996 Illegal Immigration Reform and
Responsibility Act. The Maras would engage then and now in brutal
battles with other gangs and cartels for their piece of the drug business in Central America.

   The press was all bad, and all the beach restaurants and hotels
were desperate for business. I stopped a dozen miles out of Libertad,
in better days a surfing mecca, at a small hotel. A young hippie kid
manned the front desk. He hated that El Salvador got such bad press.

Everyone writes about how dangerous it is here, he said. It isn't fair.

You have a very American accent, I said.

Yeah, man, he said, I was born in L.A. My father was deported when I was three. But it's not fair, what they say. They write about places they haven't even been! He was truly pained, rubbing his sparse beard and shaking his head. Where are the drugs? he asked. Where are the drug gangs? Not here! Not anywhere I go! Do you see drugs? Do you see gangbangers?

I didn't, but the drugs were moving through, and the murder rate was almost twenty times higher than in the United States, with homicide rates second, globally, only to Honduras, where much of the violence, too, was also the result of Mara Salvatrucha.

Like Guatemala (and Honduras and Nicaragua), at least a quarter of El Salvador's population lives overseas, a good portion of that in Los Angeles, and another quarter gets the majority of its income from those overseas workers. Between that and the American drug trade, the entire region functions as a kind of poverty-stricken American suburb, with many people living in corrugated tin slums or barely electrified villages.

Another Los Angeles export is Pentecostalism. In the small mountain town of Nahuizalco, during a somewhat incoherent set of discussions with the town *boracho*, drunk already at noon, I heard what sounded like a band practicing. I walked toward the sound of an electric guitar until I came to a freshly painted blue building on the outskirts. In white paint, in neat block letters, the building announced it was Tabernaculo Biblico Bautista Amigos de Israel, with a Star of David on one end and a menorah on the other. I stuck my head in and found a band made up of pretty talented high school and junior high kids. I acted as the band's Annie Leibovitz, photographing each of them from several angles as they played. They loved it, feeling a bit like rock stars, and we talked a little about music, about Santana, who had clearly influenced the remarkably talented twelve-year-old guitar player, and about life in their small town. They played for services at the church, and they tried to explain to me why the place was decorated with menorahs and Stars of David, only, it seemed to me, to realize they didn't know.

The minister came in and said he welcomed my fellowship, my *comunión*, my *confraternidad*. He told me that this was a branch of the largest evangelical church in San Salvador, one that has temples in Los Angeles and other American cities as well. I asked what the name meant, why Israel, and he said that in the end times the biblical prophesies will be fulfilled, and Jesus will return and bring his children into heaven. *Pero*, he said, seeing that I wasn't quite following the reasoning, this was much less important than what the church did for people day to day, its importance to people's lives, the confraternidad.

I walked back toward town and passed a small bodega, the size of a prison cell, that had laundry soap, rice, a few boxes of vegetables, sodas, and an assortment of automatic weapons for sale.

Signs hanging over the central square next to the cathedral in San Salvador have images of revolvers and AK-47s with a circle with a line through it—no guns allowed in the park. I wondered how they would enforce that.

But while it is true that in 2014 a Mara member shot a man and his two young sons because he was momentarily blocking a street that the gangster wanted to drive down, most of the murder is, as we say, gang related—it is part of a battle for territory and the resulting endless cycles of retribution, including retribution against the police and justice system. The kid in La Libertad was right. Citizens rarely get drawn in, and tourists less so. A few Americans are killed each year in the country, but most have some dealings with the gangs.

You are a writer, the kid said to me, in his almost empty beachside hotel. Tell them it isn't true. Tell them the truth, that this is a beautiful place, a good place to be a tourist.

THE WILD WEST
Ocopateque-Yamaranguila, Honduras

The Wild West of Honduras, entering from Citalá, El Salvador, just below Ocopateque, is cowboy country and wide open. Saddled horses wait outside the doors of lonely stucco compounds dotted through the agricultural plains and the dry, wooded mountains. Three hours of mountain road and you come to Copán Ruinas, near the Guatemalan border, a Mayan complex of extraordinary proportions that has been largely excavated, including an entire brightly colored (and it seemed to me suspiciously colored) underground temple, now preserved under a museum roof.

The indigenous people in these mountains are no longer the Maya, but the Lenca, a culture of strong women, at least in part because so many of the men are economic migrants. I stopped to talk to a couple of women in their forties, sturdy women with clear, strong eyes. Their Spanish wasn't great, but after I took their pictures, one of them said, in Spanish, Finally, now, I'm a model! and I admitted that yes, she was. Her friend smiled slightly—they are women who live tough lives, scraping the necessities out of what was available, and though not often given to easy amusement, I guessed, they were not opposed to it, either.

Through most of the Lencan mountains, the roads are gravel and steep, the peaks often in the clouds, and machetes and oxen do a lot of work. There were times, as I wandered up and down the washed-out roads, that I had to decide whether to press on or turn back, and

it was clear that I was making an irrevocable decision, that the hill
I was considering going down was too steep and rutted for my little
car to get back up. One day at around noon, I arrived in Yamaranguila, a town midway along the ridge that runs from the Guatemalan
border to the semilawless capital of Tegucigalpa. Yamaranguila has
a half-dozen buildings, including an eighteenth-century church and
the home and office of the *vara alta*, the Lenca elder who acts as tribal
leader for the area. He invited me in, and I made a small offering to
what he told me was a traditional Lenca shrine, an altar crowded
with other offerings—cash, corn, ribbons, oils—and bordered with
framed pictures of Jesus, Saints Christopher and George, and a car-
toon-character clock. The vara alta was a businessman at heart, and
he had a good pitch about preserving traditional Lenca cuture. I
bought a souvenir from his shelves.

A very drunk man of thirty or so in the town square tried to talk
to me but couldn't form a word. Tall, paunchy, and wide, with white
hair streaming out of a fraying straw cowboy hat, he seemed not just
temporarily incapacitated but chronically, tragically inebriated. A
sixteen-year-old girl wearing a flour-dusted apron walked by us with
a board on her head, on top of that a wad of bread dough wrapped in
a cloth. She, like most of the young women in the small towns, would
not look me in the eye. A man rode by on an only partially broken
young horse; the horse danced wildly half sideways across the cobblestones. He was trying to get it calmed down, and enjoying it. Other
than that, the town was quiet.

I headed north, where back in the countryside a man and his son
gathered firewood and lashed it to a packhorse. Another man was
bringing larger logs home in a cart pulled by enormous, sullen oxen.
Such a mix of times and cultures—even though there is little left of
the culture that built the Mayan pyramids, and despite the inflated
rubber tires on the oxcart and the assorted T-shirts and jeans,
ancient ways of life persevered. Will this continue to survive? I asked
the Lencan elder. Will the old ways last another fifty years? Yes, he
said. You can help. He pointed to the donation box for his museum.
He wore a cowboy hat and a short-sleeved Oxford shirt.

WHY DON'T THEY HATE US?

Grenada, Nicaragua

Hey, what you *want*, man? he asked me, in the square in Grenada, friendly. I had been fumbling with my Spanish a bit, trying to buy a popsicle from a woman who was sitting on a stool under a faded, striped umbrella, leaning on her refrigerated cart. She had shop-curled hair, slightly bleached, and she was clearly glad to see the man. She didn't care so much about me—she was sure she would sell me something, or not, no big deal—but him, she was happy to see. They flirted a little, in an old groove. He was a man women liked, midthirties, good-looking enough, not too good-looking, and he cut a *buen figura*, as they say—he attracted attention, had an easy patter, loud but not too loud, knew how to hold the spotlight, an easy laugh, fun. She was a little older than he was, maybe just past forty, knew what was what, and flirted back in a way that said she knew men well. Whether or not he could back up the implied promise of his brash innuendoes, she knew how to up the ante, and they both knew how to enjoy the promise itself.

I don't know, what does she have? I asked.

¡Él dice, no sé lo que tiene! ¡Pobre niño! he said, winking, making fun of me while flirting some more—*poor boy, he doesn't know what you've got!*—and they both laughed.

I meant what kind of ice cream, I said.

I know, man, just playing. Coconut or lemon.

Coco, I said, and she passed me one. I was going to offer to buy him one too, but he was drinking a beer from a brown bottle. He pointed to a horse and buggy at the curb.

You want a tour of the old city? he asked.

I really don't, I said. Thanks.

Yeah, you ain't the type, he said, I see that. But I tell you, man, it's tough here now, no tourists.

He dropped his beer bottle in a beat-up trashcan and winked at the woman. She pulled another from her cart, and I handed her a bill to pay for it. He tipped the top of the bottle to his forehead in salute. I asked him where he got his English.

Washington, D.C., bro, he said. Bike courier. Six years.

Explain something to me, then, I said. Why don't people hate us here? Why don't they hate Americans, I mean.

What for?

Well, for instance, the Contras.

Here's the thing, man, he said. I was like eleven or twelve during the war, and—he stopped and asked the woman, *¿Quieres una cerveza para ti mami?* She smiled coyly and said no, a beer was *not* what she wanted, he winked at her, wagged his finger to say *naughty girl*, and smiled back.

We were all hiding in basements and shit, he said, bombs falling, and you have to see it, back then, there was nothing like today. Nobody had TV—I mean, rich people had TV, but not people—and the newspapers, well, nobody read them. The left-wing papers blame everything on the U.S., and the right-wing papers blame everything on Castro, everybody thought, okay, whatever, we don't know. I mean, *I* know the history *now*, but I lived in D.C. for six years, man. Most people here still don't know what went down. They never been out of this town, and it ain't like they doing research.

The colonial square buzzed lazily around us, a few boys kicked a soccer ball past, the other horse-and-buggy drivers were hanging, talking to each other. The used-book man straightened his yellowed stock. The souvenir sellers fanned themselves. No tourists were in sight.

Don't they teach it in school? I asked. There are the Sandinista murals still around, I see. The murals were fading and peeling most places, but they were still visible. The Sandinistas must like the history being taught, I said.

Yeah, well, Sandinistas, right. People don't look to them for *truth*, man, besides, people ain't looking for history, they looking for a *job*.

He took a swig of his beer. His horse flopped its tail back and forth, lazily.

Anyway, think about it, he said. America ain't the enemy, my man, America is the *goal*. We hear about your economic troubles, you know: American economy in decline! But whatever you got, we got worse. You want to see an economy in decline, you come to Nicaragua, am I right? Hate America? I tell you, if Barack Obama said, tomorrow, that the doors were open?—he had to stop and laugh—all these countries, Nicaragua, Honduras, El Salvador, all these countries be *empty*, man.

Two men in their eighties sat on the edges of folding chairs playing chess. Three other men, as old or older, watched. The colonial buildings had been patched and painted a bit in expectation of tourists, but they still sagged and wrinkled pathetically. Half the park's shrubbery was withered, the rest thin. It was all pretty grim.

But I'm glad I'm back, he said. The horse and buggy is good, when there are enough tourists. I like to talk, I get good tips. But now there aren't many tourists. Everyone is afraid of the violence, they say. But look around. Where is the violence? It's just drug dealers killing each other, he said. I wish people knew that here in Granada, things ain't so bad.

Something on the chessboard caused a good-natured ruckus—all the old men yelling and laughing—and he dropped his beer bottle in the trash, said to the woman with a good-natured leer, ¡Mami, una día!, and to me said, It's true, one day, she'll be mine! wagged his finger at her, smiled at me, and went to kibitz with the chess players. The ice cream vendor shook her head, mock-dolefully, still flush with his attention. Some day, she seemed to be thinking. Who ever knows?

THE CHURCH BELLS OF QUITO

Quito, Ecuador

I woke up several times during the night, in my apartment off the Plaza de Santo Dominga, to the church bells ringing. There is no story here. The apartment was owned by a German who had lived there for thirty-five years. He loved Ecuador, he said, always had. He explained, carefully, pointing to a map, that I could walk on this road but not on that one—too dangerous, even if it is only a block away. Be careful too, he said, about the altitude; especially be careful if you drink—the altitude multiplies the effect.

Some of the churches had bells that hit on the hour, some were ten minutes early, some a bit late. So they would overlap, one or the other ringing for fifteen or twenty minutes each hour. They all sounded slightly, or more than slightly, out of tune. Dogs barked in response the entire time. In the mornings the cocks crowed in the interim.

Quito is at 9,300 feet, and the air is thin. An aerial tramway takes you up to 13,500 feet, higher than all but a handful of summits in the United States, and from up there, the city, spread out in its valley below, is a pattern of gray. It is hard to pick out the churches. On the ground they are everywhere, and one can navigate the streets by them, but they are otherwise unimportant, not visited very much. Very few people attend mass. The bells ring all day, but it is only after sunset that they truly seem to come alive, and their peals command the night as the streets empty.

I was talking to the German one evening when another guest, from Belgium, came back from a walk into town. He looked like an accountant on his day off, wearing a plaid, short-sleeved shirt. He was quite drunk, in the style of the teetotaling bachelor uncle at the wedding of his favorite niece. He was weaving, losing his balance, and seemed completely unaware that he was drunk. He was just happy. The German told him to be careful. The Belgian accountant looked momentarily confused, but then said, again, very cheerfully, Well, good night!

He fumbled with his keys while the bells started their sour pealing once more.

THE SALT FLATS

Uyuni, Bolivia

Surreally flat, monstrously white, the landscape escapes into the horizon without a trace. On the edge, a single hotel, itself made of salt: bricks of salt form the walls, while loose salt, chunks, the size used to melt snow in New England, form the floors. Instead of vacuuming, the staff rakes the floors in the rooms and hallways.

Nothing grows, of course, for a hundred miles. The flats sit at twelve thousand feet. It is hard to breath. The average temperature at night is below freezing, year round. It receives zero inches of rain eight months a year. It is inhospitable.

The desk clerk was young, Indio, with black, black hair and pointed cheekbones.

Do you want standard room, he asked, or deluxe?

I think standard, I said. What is the difference?

Standard faces the back, deluxe the front.

Huh, I said. How much is the deluxe?

I'm sorry, I don't have deluxe room left. Had he watched Groucho Marx movies? No, he was serious.

It seemed unlikely that the place was full—it felt empty, but it was still day, and perhaps everyone was out in the flats.

That's too bad.

No, okay, here is one, he said, finding something in his book. It didn't cost much more, and the whole point was to see the salt flats, so I took it. He recorded my passport and I paid, and he handed the key to a young woman, who might have been his younger sister, and she walked me down the long salt hallways to the room. They were children really, the entire staff, all looking to be less than twenty, and they had a touching earnestness about doing their jobs. When I got in, the only view was of a mound of dirt in front of the window. Above it, the blank sky.

Well, this is not so good, I said, and she had no reaction. I said it again in Spanish and she shrugged. I trudged with her back to the front desk and asked her brother if there was another room.

What is the problem?

I'm sorry, I don't want to be difficult, I said. There is no view.

Ah. It was clear he didn't consider the view particularly important. I wondered how that was possible; didn't he sell rooms every day based on their view?

He searched through his books again and handed his sister another key. We trudged again, walked twice as far. The rooms in the center of the hotel had a kind of veranda, each with its own fireplace and furniture, for viewing the flats, with the sleeping part of the room on the other side of the hallway. These were actual deluxe rooms. European and Japanese tourists were lounging in a few of them.

We got to the second room, and it had a bit of a view. There was a pile of construction debris that took up most of it, but to the right of that I could see the flats. Good enough. I tipped the young woman and went out to walk toward the flats as the sun set and the temperature dropped fast.

To see the salt flats is to want to walk into them, to wander toward the invisible distance, where the horizon—hard to say whether it is the salt or sky—turns a light gray that is almost pink in the morning and evening. A wild, dainty vicuña stood by the pitted road, her thick almond fur fluttering in the wind, staring with her deep black eyes as if she too were drawn toward the blankness.

BEING A WHORE IN ECUADOR

Quilotoa Loop, Ecuador

Somewhere along the four hours of chunky dirt road from Sigchos
to Toacazo, I came across four kids walking home from school. Most
indígenas in Ecuador don't like to have their picture taken, and
when I asked, by raising my eyebrows hopefully and pointing to my
camera, they usually said no. The farther away from tourist routes,
though, the more likely a yes, and this switchbacked, dusty route,
forsworn by most tourists heading to Quilotoa Crater for the paved
southern route out of Latacunga, is as remote as can be. It used to be
part of what was known as the Quilotoa Loop, back when all Ecuador
had was bad road. But ever since the southern route was paved, few
people do the loop anymore, and the scattered farms are now even
more remote than they were thirty and fifty years ago, the Quich-
ua-speaking kids less likely to see a tourist.

When I stopped to ask these kids about a picture, they ran to the
car and hopped in—two boys and two girls, all between six and ten,
along with two sickly puppies—and I figured, okay, that's what it
means when a car stops along this road, twelve thousand feet in the
air in the middle of nowhere: it's an offer of a ride. I took them a few
miles, and their Spanish seemed if anything worse than mine, or so
heavily accented and so polyglot that I couldn't follow a thing they
were saying. When they motioned me that it was time to stop, they
got out, and I did too. I did the standard ask, the raised eyebrow and
all, and, they said no, no foto, and laughed and started to run.

Hey! I said. ¡No es bueno! I gave you a ride! Yo ayudo ustedes!

The tense was wrong, but they knew I said something about helping them, and they relented, stopped, and let me approach. Sure enough, once we got into the rhythm of it, them mugging for the camera, then crowding in to see the screen, then mugging again, they had fun, laughing and ribbing each other. Then the oldest girl, the ten-year-old, smiled, said something to the others, and they all ran away. Before disappearing down a steep valley, she turned and gave me the finger, and they all laughed uproariously and fell on each other and the puppies rolling down the hill toward home.

An hour later, another couple of kids were walking, and I rolled down my window, gesturing to my camera. They seemed a little frightened, but they nodded okay. One girl was five or six and her sister a few years older, both dressed Indian style, not in school uniforms, both short, small for their age. I stayed in the car, and they stood still for a minute while I snapped from the window. They never smiled. After a couple snaps, they refused my offer to show them the pictures and started walking again. A few steps along, the younger girl turned to me, still stone-faced, and said, quietly, before turning away again:

Puta.

She then walked without hurry, determined, along the road.

¿Que? I asked, not believing I heard her right, because why would she call me a whore? A *whore? ¿Porque puta?* I called after her.

She looked back at me, still emotionless, flinty, her short, squat frame tense but resolute in her tough woolen clothes, and said it again, even more quietly, almost as if talking to herself:

Puta.

Then she turned, determined, and walked slowly away.

BEACH
Boca Chica, Dominican Republic

In the 1960s, Boca Chica, a stretch of sand some thirty miles east of Santo Domingo, the capital, was a private beach, with a couple of vacation houses held by the DR's wealthiest families nearby, and into the 1970s it remained an important playground for the well-to-do. Thirty-five years later the beach was a people's beach, a working-class beach, and not kept very well.

The town is a muddy dump, and an open-air brothel. Women, girls really, grab you on the street as you try to walk through town, grab your crotch, and with a lot of papi this and papi that and eyelash batting promise you the best time of your life. It is the most aggressive solicitation on the globe, even at noon, even with little kids running around, families walking by. A girl who couldn't have been more than fifteen grabbed me by the arm and planted her feet in the dirt of the road like a mule refusing to budge, and giggled as she refused to let go, playing at it more like a girl than a woman—pretending she was being impetuous rather than violent. A boy of about seven came over to where she was trying to drag me into a bar, looked up at my face with youthful curiosity—*what does a man do in such a situation?*—saw my distress, and ran away giggling. An older women sweeping cigarette butts off the rough wooden floor of the open-sided bar watched the struggle and laughed too. Everyone, in fact, seemed to be having a good time in this muddy, godforsaken place.

But they also seemed as if they weren't, really, like the laughter was forced, defensive, the giggling nervous or strategic. There is a certain kind of businesslike realism in some red-light districts around the world, especially those uninfected by Christian ideas of the sins of the flesh, as in Thailand, where one doesn't immediately feel desolation just because there is a room or two full of prostitutes spilling out into the street—places where everyone can remain somewhat respectful, where humiliation for one or more of the parties is not a necessary part of the package. Boca Chica is somewhere in between, with a Latin American embrace of sexuality mitigating, somewhat, the Catholic guilt. But it is also tinged with desperation, because people are poor, and catching a trick can make the difference between someone getting enough to eat or not, perhaps between getting out of this mess or not.

Once I made it out of the center of town without succumbing to the wiles or arm wrestling of the women, I was hounded by a group of boys asking for money. They followed me all the way to my car, crowding me, trying to pick my pockets, and wouldn't let me close my door. I had to start driving down the street before they finally fell away, laughing. It felt like a taunt, though, not like fun. The desperation was real.

The thing that interested me the most was that the beach—which was dirty, the water not great, a crappy beach, really—was filled with families, all of whom had to walk through the same gauntlet. The thing that I couldn't stop thinking was, *this is normal*, however exceptional it all seemed to me. Perhaps my own primary sin of pride is feeling that nothing human is foreign to me, that as a cosmopolitan person I don't judge, that I cannot be surprised or thrown off my game by the varieties of human experience. I've broken bread with racists in South Africa and criminals of various stripes in the United States and drug dealers here and there, and these were far from the first prostitutes I've met or the first economic crimes against people's humanity I'd witnessed. I should not, by rights, have been so shaken by this experience, made so sorrowful, but I was. *This is normal*, I told myself, but it didn't help.

CULTURE UNDER CASTRO
Havana, Cuba

The annual film festival in the Dominican Republic had a contingent from Cuba I fell in with, and despite my marginal linguistic skills, we managed to have some interesting conversations. There were a couple of filmmakers, a woman from the Cuban film commission, and a couple of academics, including a literature professor from the University of Havana with better English than my Spanish. We exchanged cards, and a year later, as I was making my way to Havana, I sent the lit prof a couple of emails, saying I'd love to meet up, have lunch or dinner if she could.

When I heard nothing, I wondered about internet censoring but didn't think too much about it. Walking past the university once I arrived, though, I decided to drop in and try an office. The university was in a building that, like the famous cars on the street, was far from new, but had been kept up well. It was the kind of building we expect in urban high schools in the United States—everything bare bones, outdated, and people busy, both students and staff, without much hanging out going on.

Signage was largely nonexistent, but by asking some custodial staff I managed to find a literature department office and, eventually, the professor. She was surprised and not, it seemed, that happy to see me. I felt, all of a sudden, like a stalker. She was clearly a little nervous, and I kept thinking *this is why you never make professional contacts when you travel, Tom, people don't want to see you! What were you thinking?* But she brought me into the office she shared with two other professors and we sat down for a chat. Her colleagues were both in their thirties too, and they all had specialties in European, American, and Latin American literature. I asked about their professional lives, what the state of literary writing and literary studies was, how their libraries were. The libraries, they said, were terrible, and when they traveled, they bought as many books as they could, and everyone in the system shared them. Most of their reading, they said, was of photocopies of books, not the books themselves.

Really, we only catch up with theory and scholarship when we travel, one said. It is not ideal. But then we are a poor country—that our library is not what it might be is not surprising.

One showed me the books he was reading at the moment, both binder-clipped stacks of double-sided photocopied sheets, one by Michel de Certeau and one by M. M. Bakhtin.

I was a fan of both writers, and we talked literary theory for a half hour, and then they discussed their research as the day came to a close.

I asked whether we might meet for dinner, but all three begged off, all with convincing enough reasons—children, work—but I couldn't help but think they were afraid to be in public with me. Since the woman I met in the DR had been very friendly there and had been actively engaged in the discussion we just had, I decided it wasn't me, it was something else—they all begged off immediately, reflexively, it seemed. They must, I decided, be wary of fraternizing with an American. The very fact I hadn't shown up through official channels might be part of the problem.

As I wandered around Havana the following days, that impression grew. I was talking to a young man briefly, and he stopped, after a minute, looked down, and turned away.

Could you please step inside this shop with me? he said, without turning around, and walked into a bodega. I followed.

Why did we do that? I asked.

The cameras, he said. They will want to know what we talked about, why I was talking to you. It will just be trouble for me.

Cameras?

Yes, downtown here, every street there are cameras. They know where you are going, who you are talking to.

It happened once again, with a young woman. She asked me not to follow too close but to please join her in a hotel lobby. I did, and she apologized and explained that she was a prostitute, and soliciting foreigners was a crime, so she couldn't do it front of the cameras. That made sense and didn't require massive political repression as an explanation. But the idea that the cameras were that prevalent, and that people had dealt, personally, with fallout from being seen by the cameras—it wasn't paranoia, apparently, it was fear.

The next day, I heard a band practicing near my hotel and introduced myself. I went with them to a club gig—a great group of ten very young musicians who played a mix of *son*—the Cuban version of salsa—and funk and hip-hop. They were extremely comfortable on stage, extremely talented. I spent some time talking to a woman in the audience who was a schoolteacher. She said I should see some other culture, and that tomorrow night the Cuban National Ballet was at the Great Theatre, one of the grand old halls downtown. She would get me a ticket at the local price, which was five cents.

I met her there the next night and went to the show, a tribute to Alicia Alonso, who founded the company in 1948. After the revolution, Castro subsidized the ballet (and other arts) and kept Alonso as the director. The building was rich in wood and velvet, out of time, and when Alonso came in, it was like a scene from *Sunset Boulevard*. She looked ancient and dogged in heavy white makeup and a turban. Her husband had a head like Jorge Luis Borges's and was clearly her chief factotum. When the crowd saw her come in, they hopped to their feet and gave her a long ovation. She took it as her due. She was ninety years old. She still ran the ballet.

The dancing was all from her choreography and not particularly interesting. The dancers were good, but none were exceptional. The woman who brought me was thrilled to be sitting so near Alonso.

This is very special for me, she said, to see her so close like that. She is a legend in Cuba.

Only five cents! I said.

Yes, the government pays. This is a good thing, she said.

As we walked back from the theater, I asked her why she wasn't afraid to be seen with me.

Why should I be? she asked, and laughed. Are you a famous American spy?

No, I said, but I told her the story of my university professor, and how she seemed to be afraid to talk to me, and about the kids downtown.

Well, like you said, one was a prostitute—what did the other one want?

To practice his English.

I don't think so.

Why do you say that?

I don't think he is afraid to practice his English in front of the cameras. Did he offer to take you somewhere?

No, he gave me his cell number, said to let him know if I needed anything. It seemed innocent enough.

Yes, well, he is not someone to play with, she said.

Huh. The paranoia was paranoia, then.

So why, I asked, why would the professors not have dinner with me?

To go out to dinner, to one of the restaurants, at a hotel?—this is not something working people can do. I think maybe they were embarrassed to tell you they could not afford such a thing.

I would have taken them! I said.

Yes, but they could not know—and they have some pride, I think. Cubans are very proud. Too proud to be afraid of cameras! She laughed. We are here—my house is that way, your hotel is just there. Let's wave to the cameras—and she waved in all four directions—and say goodnight, and hope for better days for Cuba!

CAFÉ LA POESÍA

Buenos Aires, Argentina

San Telmo is the Greenwich Village of Buenos Aires, and it is similarly hard for an outsider to tell some of the tourist places from the
more or less local ones. The café bar La Poesía was, in fact, full of
writers, even if some of them were American. The piano player was
a studious young man with a beard and stacks of sheet music, each
composition folded out five or seven times so there was no need to
turn pages. He was good, although with a too-heavy foot on the sus-
tain pedal, and not as good as his acordeonista, also bearded, who
had an incredible touch and fluidity on his diatonic accordion, and
who never once looked at the music. When he played, the tango did
what it is meant to do—it created immediate longing.

At the table next to me, a guy who just had to be a poet, in his middle forties, with lots of gray—although the gray hairs were still in the
minority in the thick mop on his head, perhaps a majority in the full
beard—sat with a woman considerably younger, and he did almost all
the talking. In fact, all the talking. I started to assume he was a professor. She was rapt, and he clearly wanted to keep her that way.

There were two young guys, slouched at a table reading literary
paperbacks—you could tell they were literary from the size, the heft,
and the lack of gloss or graphics on the covers—and they seemed
very much at home. Both were blondish and one wore a beard; the
waiters had beards, as did the other customers, it was a bearded
place. One of those beautiful, aquiline Argentine men in their seven-

ties, all of whom, whatever they might do for a living, look like intellectuals, with a gray artistic swoop of a mane, a trimmed-to-a-point gray beard, and no body fat whatsoever, chatted with a rounder friend, who was also, by proximity and intensity, an intellectual, with a goatee. A group of middle-aged American tourists were at another table, a German couple sat behind me, and a large group of young Argentine friends had pulled tables together on the opposite wall. That wall, like all the others, was covered with old photos of writers, most of whom I'd never heard of, some framed lyric poems, and a few cartoons, all in a Gertrude Stein–like arrangement, filling the entire available space.

A second young woman came in, who looked to be eighteen, and cheek-kissed the poet and his student/mentee. The poet made a place for her at the table and then turned his entire attention to her. She talked a bit but was very shy, and to help her out perhaps, he started talking. Eventually, the first woman, who I could see then was in her mid to late twenties, began to look a bit embarrassed and got up to go, making a brave smiling face of it. The professor barely acknowledged that she left, but the younger woman noted it by taking over her chair across from the poet. As far as I could tell, she never said another word. He leaned across the table toward her and orated a torrent. With the music going I couldn't quite catch any of it. What an age for a man!—the middle forties—he feels old and denies it, he knows better than to chase approval but can't help himself, he longs for bliss and finds humiliation instead, but in the throes of his desperate quest he is flush with energy and possibility. So this man, an Argentine Phillip Roth character. His glasses were expensive. He wore a scarf.

Two more young women came in, one a brunette who proceeded to throw an enormous head of highlighted curls around in a very Argentinian way and scan the room for the admiration she felt her due; she had an improbably tiny waist and had tied off her loose T-shirt so everyone could know. Her friend was a blond gamine with an Audrey Hepburn cut, and she was both proud of and a little wary about her friend. They decided on a table just across from the poet-professor, and I wondered—are these his office hours? Or is he famous? But no, he glanced at them, and they at him, and that was that. They were not interested, and he renewed his focus on girl number two. She looked grateful.

I spent some time writing, working on a piece about a trip to Swaziland, and had a couple coffees. The poet and his mentee were still there when I left. He was talking, one hand raised in the air.

THE BLUE ECONOMY
Buenos Aires, Argentina

You are getting a decent rate, I hope, she said. You know not to go to a bank, right?

She was originally from either New York or Montreal, I couldn't remember which, as she had lived in both places, and also in Istanbul, before settling, for now, in Buenos Aires.

Yes, I read online, I said, not to use the banks. I found a cash service, a Western Union kind of place, that was pretty good. I net ten pesos to the dollar.

Oh, not bad, she said, although she was clearly unimpressed.

Not good? I knew the official rate was 7.8.

No, it's fine, and these street guys have a million tricks, so it was probably smart.

¡Cambio, cambio, cambio! is what the guys on the street called out, dozens of them at every major public place, but especially on Florida Street, where a half dozen a block ply their pesos. The white economy, as it's called—the official, taxable, and recorded economy—is shadowed, as it is anywhere, by the black market, which includes such things as criminal income and illegal, undeclared, under-the-table transactions. But in Argentina there are extra wrinkles. The blue economy, as they call it, falls somewhere between black and white. Like the trade in pesos, these informal modes of exchange are so common and quasi-legal that the going street rates are published in the daily paper alongside the official rate. There is also a gray

economy, another form of official-unofficial commerce, a necessary category because even some state employees are paid off the official books—something having to do with internal and external (as in IMF) politics, and not having the actual numbers printed in the papers. The entire country runs double books.

The problem started with the crisis of 2002, when there was a run on the banks, causing a massive crash. Inflation of more than 25 percent—again there are official and unofficial estimates—meant that nobody wanted to hold pesos. The government passed restrictions on how much people could withdraw each day, and people have been taking out the maximum every day since. Half of all Argentines' savings are now in foreign currencies in foreign banks, and another 10 to 15 percent are held in dollars or euros in mattresses or safe deposit boxes.

Estimates vary as to how much of the economy is white, blue, gray, or black.

When I bought my apartment, my friend said, which you have to do in cash—

I must have looked surprised.

Yes! she said. Can you imagine? Suitcases and suitcases! We had armed guards, they had armed guards. It was in a special place, a place designed for these things, and it had its own armed guards! Passwords, multiple gates, like an action movie! Can you imagine? Intrigue!

She is in love with tango. She dances several nights a week. She does her banking in the United States. I asked if she went to Florida Street to exchange for pesos.

No, she said, I have a guy—it's like buying drugs in New York—I know, ridiculous!—you have a guy who you have to be introduced to, through one of his customers, who he trusts, who has to vouch for you, and then you go to his apartment and do the deed there.

And the ethics of it all? There's an argument that the unofficial economy robs the commonwealth by keeping some money off the tax rolls.

I think no, that the leftists are right about this, she said. The government and the international financial system got us into this mess, and they and the banks all made their money. The informal economy is just a way for regular people to not get completely screwed. It's good for the government right now if the peso is valued at the official rate. It's bad for people. I'm a people!

My first day in the city was March 24, which is celebrated as the Day of Remembrance for Truth and Justice in Argentina, and Buenos Aires was alive with marches, troops of people in matching T-shirts carrying twenty-foot-high banners and accompanied by loosely put-together bands of various kinds, drums and horns, mostly, with food stands set up every block or so, and a combination of somber political emotions and carnival. It seemed to me that everyone was claiming to be a Peronista—the trade unions, several different political parties, some of which otherwise seemed right wing and some left. I asked her to explain.

It can't be explained, she said. At least not in the time we have. Eva Perón managed to be many things to many people when she was alive, and even more so now that she is dead. People aren't so much Peronistas as they are Eva-istas.

Whatever the reason, one legacy of the Peróns' populism seems to be that people want to get out in the streets and make a statement, that they find such protests are worth doing, that it is worth their time and considerable effort to get out and march, to plaster the city with political posters. I wasn't sure if it represented democracy in action or a failure of democracy, but it was thrilling to see.

My friend wasn't sure she was going to stay in Argentina.

I never decided to live anywhere forever, she said. Including here. Who knows?

Her partner at the time was a medical researcher turned tango instructor who had been running a lab studying DNA and RNA in Japan for five years before deciding he'd had enough of the rat race, threw away his PhD, and started teaching in a studio in their apartment. He was happy in Argentina and therefore so was she, for the moment.

You don't miss New York or Montreal? I asked.

No, she said. I have never known a city so alive, so artistically alive as this. It's an exhilarating place. She turned wistful, as if she were imagining someplace else, or imagining already having moved on.

I do like to tango, she said.

TANGO

San Cristobal, Argentina

The "Underground" Tango Club—that's what a young dancer called it, switching to English after she got tired of struggling with my Mexican Spanish—was scruffy and reminded me of the midwestern country music scene. It wasn't just the shoes—the dancers bring their dance shoes in shoe bags to the club and change there, like they're in a bowling league. And it wasn't just the absolute lack of attention to decor or the way only a few of the people were dressed up, more women than men of course, and even in those cases, except for the women's tango shoes, nothing looked expensive. Many of the characters were the same as you'd find in any two-step country dance hall in Iowa—men and women for whom these nights of dancing were of central importance. It would be too easy to say it was like church, but still, for the tango dancers something essential about what it means to be fully alive was happening in this out-of-the-way club, miles from downtown Buenos Aires.

I did a five-year stint in a Nashville top-forty cover band in Iowa a while back, playing keyboards, and whether it was the Red Stallion out by the highway in Coralville or the Electric Ballroom in Waterloo or the other old big band halls scattered through the corn and soybean fields (like my favorite, a place in Swisher—I don't remember the name because everyone just called it Swisher—a place that had been a roller-skating rink in the 1940s, the wooden skate surface a perfect dance floor), in all those places the locals all knew the

dances, all knew each other, and they all took dancing very seriously, passionately. There always were some dumpy-looking guys
who could really dance and some smooth older guys who otherwise
had no business grabbing young girls by the waist. And some good-
enough dancers who were naturally unthreatening, and who knew
all the rules, both social and terpsichorean, and never sat out a number. There were always one or two sharply dressed guys, probably
gay, who were the best dancers and the women's favorites, a few couples who only danced with each other, a couple of women who would
dance with each other each night, a couple of short guys dancing
with women a head or more taller, and always some pretty girls in
hot outfits who would increase the tension in the room but never go
home with anyone. The Argentinean versions of all of them were on
the floor.

This connection didn't hit me right away. The club was off in the
middle of nowhere, where Avenida San Juan hits Avenida Jujuy, several empty dark blocks from any other business, and when I said it
was my first night of tango in Argentina, the woman I was talking to
looked shocked, and she said, ¿Siempre? Ever?

Well, no, I heard a duo playing in a café, but this is my first time to
see the dancing.

But how did you find this place? she asked, incredulous. This is
very hidden. Who told you to come here?

A friend who I met in New York and lives here now—she dances
here sometimes.

Yes, because this is not for tourists! You see these people, they all
know each other. I only come once in a long time. It is almost the private club.

And that's the way it felt when I walked in. I wasn't unwelcome,
but the looks said you're on your own. There were enough hipsters
in evidence at around 11:30 PM, just before the dancing got started
around midnight, that I felt one part fly on the wall and two parts
fish out of water. The DJ would play a set of four or five tango tunes,
most of which were around three minutes, some very scratchy,
78-rpm-sounding, all old, and then put on a palate cleanser, something from another genre. These intermezzos were also dance

tunes—reggae, rock, disco, new wave—but it didn't matter. As soon as the off-genre piece started, the floor cleared. It seemed like great social engineering; nobody ever had to say, *okay, thanks, that was great, bye.* There was a prescheduled end to every pairing; once a couple hit the floor, they did four or five numbers and then retired to their separate tables, ready to recouple.

I can two-step and do a little ballroom, but the tango, for all I studied the couples on the floor, remained a mystery. That it is like sex goes without saying, and like interesting sex. The pauses are ecstatic and many, the languorous moments both proof and portent. The sinuous leg moves of the women, the face-to-face gaze, and the high hug—the woman's crooked elbow is often higher than the man's shoulder, and the man's hand is not in the small of the back, but at breast height—all of it meant that even the mediocre dancers were a pleasure to watch. And the best of them were like watching an Astaire-Rogers number, more like pairs figure skating than dancing in American clubs. The eight-beat phrases of the Argentinian tango end with a pause in the final beat, but sometimes that musical pause is used for a dancerly flourish, and sometimes it enforces a complete suspension of movement. The dancing pause is even more fun when the music is frenetic.

All the recordings were from the 1930s and even the 1920s, which is of course when American country music developed what we recognize as its classic form. I mentioned this to a guy at the bar, a guy with an unstyled beard and the standard young "alternative" hairdo, long hair pulled up tight into a top knot, a man bun, the sign of the progressive, antineoliberal, antihipster hipster.

Yes! This is country music! he said. It is *now* of course, you know, the Argentine elite's favorite music, but they *hated* it when it started. It was *bordello* music, *whorehouse* music, like your blues and jazz, *despised* by the rich, music for the *poor.* Then the Parisians picked it up, and the bourgeoisie here noticed it for the first time. If the *Parisians* hadn't made a big fuss, these bourgeois city people would *still* hate it.

He excused himself when the next tango came on and grabbed a new partner. The scratchy record called across the decades, and as in the case of American roots music, the keepers of the flame here revere the past and reject popular versions. They all had great disdain for the tango shows in the central city, the places where tourists see a rigidified, codified, commercialized version, they say, not the real thing. For the people out past Avenida Jujuy at 3 AM, Astor Piazzolla was a sellout, and the best music was not only from the past, it was from the deep past, from the dawn of the form, from the dawn of the country's recording industry.

A couple of stars were in attendance that night, people who were known to be among the best dancers in the country, and when they took the floor it cleared, people retreating to the chairs along the walls or just sitting down cross-legged in front of the tables to watch and exclaim at particularly impressive moves.

The performers carried themselves with the seriousness their almost sacred status required, knowing that, in their perfection, the stuff that all these devotees worshipped was housed; they were the tabernacle, the ark of the covenant, and they carried within them the truth of the form, the essence of tango. He was of medium height and, like a successful actor, he managed to be his biological age of forty in attitude and maybe ten years less in appearance. She, in her five-inch heels, was taller and a few years younger. Both were impeccably groomed, and their clothes were contemporary evocations of the 1930s. As they started dancing, they hummed with thousands of kilowatts of pure charisma, a sublime balance of force and weightlessness, a representation of plenitude—physical, sexual, emotional—at once elemental and refined. They embodied not only their own deep longing but ours, and, it almost seemed, in the intensity of the moment, all of humanity's.

They danced to four songs, never flinching, never not fundamentally serious, never less than impressive, never striving, always on the edge of some ecstasy. Like Astaire and Rogers, they affected effortlessness effortlessly and danced at a level not given to mere mortals. They eschewed flashiness, did nothing pyrotechnic, broke no new ground, and yet every move of every limb, every bend of the torso, every look into each other's eyes, represented the sublime intersection of desire and its frustration, longing and fulfillment, need and promise. The crowd—I forced myself to look away and watch them too—was in thrall, mesmerized, beguiled, enchanted.

When they were done, the woman next to me said, almost wistfully, This is not a typical place. The people here, they dance every night.

INCIDENT IN THE OLD CITY
Montevideo, Uruguay

Online reports about my hotel mentioned the sketchy neighborhood, so I was forewarned. The Ciudad Vieja in Montevideo, I saw as
I arrived, doesn't just have historic buildings, it has geriatric ones,
disintegrating, with vegetation, even small trees, growing off the
ledges and out of cracks. Many are empty. The attempt to make a
tourist and yuppie paseo out of the area remains, at this point, quix-
otic. There are a few restaurants near the port, and they bustle when
a cruise ship docks. The Plaza Independencía, on the far end of the
neighborhood, has been refurbished and has some nightlife up until
around midnight.

But the rest of the old city is nothing but old. At night, the streets
are empty. As early as 8:00 PM you can walk three or four blocks
without seeing a soul, without finding an open business, restaurant,
or bar. The best place I found to eat was open for lunch only. Fear is
what empties streets like that, and when I went out at night, I went
out very light, without anything electronic, no cards, just a mini-
mum amount of cash. Even during the day, I had to be buzzed into
my hotel.

The armored trucks in Montevideo—Prosegur and Brinks—move
cash and checks around the city, followed by a car with four men.
The car is not brand new, not fancy, but painted with the company's
colors and logo. When the truck stops, two of the men jump out of
the car, one of them stays in the backseat, gun at the ready, guarding

the driver. The two gunmen establish sight lines and stand with their automatic weapons at the ready.

Then an armed guard gets out of the front of the truck and scouts in all directions. He knocks on the side door of the truck, and three more armed men come out. They have the cash bag (and automatic weapons). The four of them go to the bank door; the two from the car remain behind facing the street. At the front door of the bank, two guards come out and stay there with two of the truck guards; the other two enter the bank.

When all the business is done, the four men go back in the truck, the two extra guards return to their car, and the two vehicles race to their next stop. This level of security suggests some very dire experiences in the past, some very desperate, very determined adversaries.

But as far as I can tell, there isn't much crime now, and the statistics say the country has the lowest rate of violent crime in Latin America. I walked the ten or twelve blocks back and forth to the Plaza Independencía at night many times, early and late, and never ran into the slightest trouble, not even the signs of it. I was often the only one walking, and perhaps like a dying ecozone, the lack of targets on the streets had decimated the predators, who had to migrate elsewhere for their prey.

One evening, though, early, I stepped out of my hotel when there were still a few people in the street, still dusk, and a young kid, maybe nine years old, came up to me and said something. The Río de la Plata Spanish—with its lack of *tu* and *usted*, its *ll* and *y* sounds pronounced like a soft *g*, and its conjugation differences—was still confounding me. I said, in my Mexican Spanish, I'm sorry, what did you say? He repeated himself, and although I still didn't catch the words, I got the idea, which was that he was asking for money. His friend, who was around twelve, was circling us on a bike. The others on the street weren't paying any attention, and there were a couple of dogs in the mix, one trailing the boy on the bike. The other dog, just like the kid, was looking for handouts. I said, this time in English, I don't understand, my Spanish is bad, and kept walking. The kid was, I could see once I focused in on him for a minute, a tiny thug and had nasty energy. I walked around him, hugged the building to keep him and the bike on my same side, and started walking toward some still-open restaurants, just a half block away. My antennae were up, and so I felt him rush me and was starting to turn to face him when he said, loudly, Money! and thrust his hand into my right pants pocket.

I reflexively grabbed at his arm, and with some adrenaline going, grabbed it hard and turned, pushing him away from my body, arm's length, but not letting go, a death grip. He tried to yank his arm away, but I was in a highly mobilized state, my adrenalized fear compounded by my distress and confusion at finding myself in this violent moment, and we both realized, at exactly the same time, that I could fuck him up. *I could break his arm!* went through my head. *I have him immobilized. I am hurting him right now.* He went a bit limp, like the little pup he was, his body signaling to the alpha dog that his fight was done, and I still couldn't let go, and in fact, I squeezed harder, and he whimpered, *Shit!* I thought, *He is nine years old!* I let go, finally, and pushed him away from me, saying loudly, *LITTLE FUCKER!* and he ran off. His friend on the bike was already long gone. The little fucker. In for a bad life. Already doomed. *The little fucker.*

Eventually, I calmed down. How easy it is to flip, I thought, how easy to go animal. I found a place with grilled meat, ate some with a carafe of wine.

The little fucker was probably still hungry.

Unless he had gotten luckier.

JAZZ IN CHILE
Santiago, Chile

Coming from Buenos Aires, where live music is everywhere, and the obsession with tango is a religion, revered the way *rebetiko* is revered in Greece, and *son* in the DR, and country music in Branson, it was odd to arrive in Chile and ask where I might see live *cueca*, the Chilean national music and dance, only to be told it was impossible.

It is in September, my first cabdriver said.

September?

Yes, September, the festival.

Only then?

Yes. He shrugged. Why not, he seemed to say. He thought for a minute, and then said, We are not like Argentines with tango.

My search for live music turned up a couple of rock clubs, some big venues with large international concerts, and few clubs with music in the next few nights. A jazz place called Thelonious on Avenida Bombero Núñez, on the other side of the river, seemed like the best bet. The show, the website said, was at 8:00 PM.

I walked the couple miles toward the club in the summer evening so I could see the neighborhood before it got too dark. Mural-like graffiti was everywhere, and all the local businesses—Bombero Núñez is a slightly run-down arty district—have decided to join instead of fight and got artists to paint their buildings. Wild colors, surrealistic collages of images, superb. I found a small café and had a decent meal.

I didn't have high hopes for the Diego Riedemann Trio. In Argentina, my one bad night was at a jazz club, where the band did lackluster imitations of Chuck Mangione and didn't seem entirely clear about the idea of soloing. I'm told there is, in fact, better jazz in Buenos Aires, but the crowded upscale audience, not tourists, were appreciative, which suggests the bar is low. The emptiness of the room, when I got to Thelonious, also didn't bode well, nor did the lack of a stage or the fact that the band was dressed like they were gathering for a rehearsal in somebody's basement—T-shirts and jeans that looked like they had already seen a long day, or worse. They stood looking at each other instead of the audience of four people. Maybe that would have been too depressing. Maybe they were all channeling Miles Davis.

When they started playing, though, they astounded me. The guitarist had taken the best of Pat Metheny and given it all Wes Montgomery's pure tone and discipline, half old school and half new school, or maybe it was post school. The bass player was one of the best accompanists I've heard on any instrument—the way he filled and prodded, syncopated, and responded and reinterpreted, and—I was in heaven. At first I thought the drummer was too busy—he did the craziest counterrhythms and the most unexpected quotations of other genres—but it was because I was expecting him to be playing a supporting part, and he wasn't; he was an equal with the other two, and they had obviously all agreed that that was the idea. All three had enormous ears and were in a conversation of such speed and range and complexity that it seemed impossible, sometimes, that they would be able to get themselves out of whatever jam they were getting themselves into or off the cliff where they teetered, all three playing in the gaps of the gaps of the gaps of the original song. One song, they announced, was Ellington. Okay, maybe it was.

They were incredibly smart, musically, but it wasn't like math rock either, they were not going after cerebral nerd points. Everything was so *smooth*—the guitarist could trail off a series of chords—full of color tones, ascending for more than seemed possible given the finite neck of his instrument—and be playing them, a mile a minute, in a fade that finally made it feel like he was stroking a cat softly rather than playing an electric guitar. They were deep in the pocket, emotional, joyous, very happily focused on the groove, appreciating each other. When jazz fails, like the week before in Buenos Aires, it is often because it is being presented instead of being listened to by the band. On these exceptional nights, the band can almost seem surprised by what their instruments are doing.

And their playing was also astoundingly *quiet*. It would not have been too loud if they were all in a car with you. Ask anyone who has played with a drummer and electric guitar player—that doesn't happen very often.

I got in a conversation with the other guy sitting at the bar, who turned out to be guitar player himself. He too was thrilled.

These guys, he said, they are the best in Chile.

After the set I bought him a glass of wine, and we talked about his music and his day job. He had moved to Buenos Aires for a few years, thinking it would be a better place to be a musician.

You see, he said, gesturing to the empty room, the great appreciation Santiago shows its best musicians.

So he tried Buenos Aires, but it didn't work. The economy is so tricky, he said. It is hard to break into the music scene as a foreigner and hard to make a living while you wait.

I am glad to be home, anyway, he said. Where are you staying?
I told him.
He will call you a cab, he said, nodding to the bartender.
I walked over, I said. I thought I would just walk back.
This is not a good idea, he said.
The city doesn't seem dangerous to me, I said. I walked around last night a bit.
Did you notice that the streets were empty?
In fact, all through Paraguay and Uruguay and Montevideo, I had been noticing that as early as 10 PM, streets would empty out, and by midnight I was alone with the dogs. Here in Santiago too.
Yes, last night, they were incredibly empty, I said.
Well, don't you think there might be a reason for that?
He asked the bartender to call me a cab.
On the drive home, the streets were empty.

URUGUAYAN POLITICS
Asunción, Paraguay

He held the elevator, a young man in colorful sweats, looking like he
was dressed for a soccer match. We were at a slightly shabby hotel in
Asunción, Paraguay.

What floor? he asked.

Quatro, I said.

But you speak English? Where are you from?

America, usted?

Uruguay.

Ah! I'm heading to Uruguay sometime next week.

I hate Mujica! he said in a burst.

He could see I was confused.

The politician! he said, I hate Mujica! He is only for, how do you say
this? He held his lightly bearded chin and looked up at the corner
of the elevator, tapping his foot, impatient that his vocabulary was
insufficient to his political rage. .

¿Por los ricos? I offered.

No, he said, glancing at me, clearly thinking, *okay, you don't know
who Mujica is, but he's a politician, so guessing that he is for the rich is reasonable.*

I did know Mujica, though—I just hadn't quite placed the name,
still getting used to that weird Rioplatanese, so even slower on the
uptake than I am with Mexican Spanish. Mujica is the president who
refuses to live in the presidential palace, still works his tiny farm

with his 1970s tractor. As far from the rich as can be, he was "the world's poorest president," with a net worth of $1,800, they say, continuing to live on his small, dirt-road farm outside the capital and drive a beat-up VW bug to work. A member of the armed political group the Tupamaros in the 1960s and 1970s, he spent fourteen years in jail under the military dictatorship, two of those years, it is said, at the bottom of a well. He gives 90 percent of his salary to charities.

He was famous for having legalized marijuana and for being the only world leader to rail against the global culture of consumption. He was disgusted by the business suit and refused to wear one: Why do we have to dress like English gentlemen? he asked in an interview. That's the suit that industrialization imposed on the world! Even the Japanese had to abandon their kimonos to have prestige in the world. We all have to dress up like monkeys with ties!

Mujica, I said. He's the farmer, right? He's left wing?

Left, so he says! But politicos, they are all the same.

They are all corrupt? I said.

Yes, all the same.

The papers make him seem popular.

No, the man in the tracksuit said. He is only loved by his own party.

We had come to his floor.

You will enjoy my country, he said. It is very beautiful.

I thanked him and went to my room, checked my email and the papers. Mujica had announced that morning that he would take detainees from Guantanamo and allow them to live freely in Uruguay. I replayed my conversation in the elevator and wondered—was the Uruguayan mad about that? He had blurted out his dislike when I said I was American. I looked for him the next day at breakfast, but he wasn't there. If he was mad about it, why? Because Mujica was playing to some anti-American base, and this guy liked Americans? He seemed friendly toward me. Anti-Americanism can be thick in the air, but he had been light, except for his anger directed across the bay. Or was it because he thought Mujica was helping America by taking the detainees off our hands and putting his own country at risk? I would never know.

When I got to Uruguay, I asked a dozen people what they thought of Mujica's offer to take the U.S. prisoners. None of them had heard about it. They almost all loved Mujica. I asked them why the man I met would have been so mad.

Was his name Lacalle? One man asked. It was a joke. Lacalle was who Mujica beat in the last election.

Another offered his rebel past. He was Tupamaro, she said. The Tupamaros were a guerrilla group that kidnapped and assassinated people in the early 1970s. If your father is killed by Tupamaros, she said, you don't forget.

But the man in the elevator had wanted me to understand that he was angry at Mujica. He could have said *he murdered my father*. But he didn't. He got off the elevator shaking his head, like he knew he had failed to explain, and that that was somehow Mujica's fault, too. He turned as the doors were closing, smiled, and said, in English, nice to meet you.

DUTCH SOUTH AMERICA

Paramaribo–Pokigron, Suriname

I was in South America, but the language and the architecture were
Dutch. I was in a tapas restaurant. The music was archival American blues, all pre-1930, much of it I hadn't heard before, and it's a
music I know fairly well. The wine by the glass was from Argentina,
Bordeaux, Spain, California, and Italy. The city has a daily Chinese
newspaper and a Chinese TV station, also a Hindi TV station. The
people were a mix of Amerindian, Sumatran, Indian, African, and
Dutch, often in a single person. New deepwater oil harvesting and
industrial gold mining had pumped up the economy in a few short
years, bringing roughnecks from Mississippi and turning the capital
Paramaribo from a mud-road wilderness outpost with crumbling
colonial buildings to a hustling, well-restored, well-painted cosmopolitan city, with a sizable number of late-model cars. The restaurant
I was in would have been at home in Atlanta or Seville. My waitress,
Jordan, who was around twenty, gave me her email address, which
began Hello_Georgeous@—, it was, she said from *Alvin and the Chipmunks*; when Alvin gets a box of chocolates, he opens it and says,
"Hello, Gorgeous!"

This, she said, I found *so* funny. I made the address when I was
fourteen.

The Guyanas—former British (now Guyana), French (still French
Guiana), and Dutch (Suriname)—all bear their colonial inheritance in
obvious ways (the official language of each is the colonial language,

for instance) and less obvious ways, and traveling through them feels like visiting a postcolonial laboratory. They share the same geography, the Atlantic on their northern border, the Amazon on the southern, crisscrossed by rivers. They have similar demographics, with the majority of the population in the capital city, and most of the rest along the Atlantic coast, and they have some similar social and economic issues (racial divides, rural poverty).

They also have some striking differences. Guyana's colonial buildings are still rotting in the dirty capital, while French Guiana's capital has kept them up and made them part of its tourist industry. French Guiana is still part of France, spends euros and votes in French elections, has European infrastructure, forty-euro cabs from the airport, and French pastry and tartare in the cafés. Suriname is between the two, geographically and economically; its capital city, Paramaribo, is sprucing itself up rapidly—with pockets of bourgeois cosmopolitanism like this tapas restaurant—while the countryside remains, except for some ecotourism lodges, scattered extraction industries, and otherwise bare subsistence.

Marianne, the woman who ran the breakfast kitchen for my small hotel in Paramaribo, or Parbo, as it is called, was around forty and had worked in Belgium, the Netherlands, and France. I asked her which was her favorite place, and she said, with pride, Suriname! I was surprised, I said, to find Paramaribo, the capital, so clean and modern and safe. The guidebooks had led me to believe that everything would be a mess, that even in the day one had to be vigilant against theft, that there would be minimal services.

No! she said. Of course, if you go around, at night, with gold everywhere—she mimed arms weighed down with dozens of bracelets and necklaces—and big camera sticking out, then, she shrugged, smiling, then it is just fishing! Yes, like being a fish! This is asking for trouble! And this happens anywhere! Paris, anywhere.

I asked if she liked Paris, if she felt any antiforeigner sentiment there.

Yes, they are very national, she said. They will only speak French to you. They know English, but they only speak French, and they know you can't understand! She smiled. Yes, she said. They don't like foreign.

Everywhere in Suriname, from the capital to the farthest flung villages, the grocery stores (and many other businesses) are owned by Chinese families—most called supermarkets, though really bodegas—called Qiang Ji Market or Hung Long (sorry, true) or Chan Lu Supermarket. In fact, they aren't called markets, they're called "Chinese"—as in, *you can get a bar of soap at the Chinese down the street.*

Suriname has a population of 540,000, more than half of them in and around the capital, most of the other half along the coast, and only forty thousand people live in the interior, in a space the size of Iowa or New York State. The roads don't go very far into the interior, either. After heading south from the coast they just stop, usually because they have run into a river. Pokigron, some three hours south of Paramaribo, is where the southernmost road in the country meets the Upper Suriname River, whose tributaries rise near the southern border, at the edge of Amazonia. This crossroads of sorts—travel is by car from Pokigron north and by boat south—is anchored by a "Chinese," the largest establishment in town at river's edge, next to which stands a barbershop and hair salon, and next to that a bar.

Across what is essentially a parking lot, although there weren't many cars, a couple of wooden government buildings stood closed, and a metal and engine shop was busy. Except at the bar, where a half-dozen men were drinking and laughing, people were at work: braiding hair and sweeping the porch at the barbershop, grinding a tool at the machine shop, unloading and loading the characteristic Surinamese longboats, built from rough boards, that arrived regularly; the boats seat two or three people on each of a dozen benches, an outboard motor on the back. These served the scattered Maroon and other villages on the hundreds of miles of rivers fanning out from the south.

The grocery store owner told me that the store had been operating for eighteen years. He and his parents had moved from China when he was ten—so his life was roughly divided into thirds: a third in China, a third helping his parents run the shop, and a third running it himself. The shop is a typical Chinese, with groceries and sundries, housewares, canned meat and fish, candy bars, and toiletries. He loves Suriname, he told me. Never cold. Ever any trouble? I asked. No, never, he said.

Coming out of the bar, a large, slightly bleary guy approached me and I said hello. He pointed to the image of a man on a small poster—one of those magnetic rubber things—on the side of what I assumed must be his car, a headshot of a man wearing a medal like an Olympian, with the words KOMEN PE? in block letters at the bottom. He asked if I knew who it was. I said no. He insisted I had to know. I read the two words.

You are not going to say his name? he said, slightly belligerently. He had clearly been drinking.

I said, Tell me, and then I will say it.

You really don't know this man? pointing at the picture. I looked at the man asking me, and there was a resemblance—was it him? was this a joke? A half-dozen men and a couple boys were watching now, some smiling at my distress. A young boy, maybe six, and clearly happy not to be the one who didn't get the joke for a change, was standing next to the truck, pointing at the man's face, laughing a little.

It is our president!

Ah, I said. Yes, I know the president, but I forget his name, he was president before—

No *now*! the man said. He is president now!

I mean, Boo, Boo-something, I know he is president now, but also before, his name is—

For five years! he said, still building with anger.

I figured I would just agree. Yes, I said, of course!

Dési Bouterse, he said.

Though it looks French, it is Dutch, so it sounded like Bow-turge. That's why my Boo-something didn't work.

Bouterse was famous for, among other things, the "December murders," in which thirteen prominent citizens who had criticized the military government were rounded up and summarily executed in 1982, along with a couple of his rivals in the military. He was also later convicted in absentia of drug trafficking by a Netherlands court. He remained head of the army until 1990, when he dismissed the current government by telephone, hence known as the "Telephone Coup," and named himself president. He presided over a tumultuous decade, including a full-out civil war with the Maroon populations. After being out of power for ten years, he was reelected in 2010.

He is a good president? I asked.

The best! The best president ever!

He is good for people here? I asked, taking in the whole upper Suriname River with a sweep of the hand.

He is the best president for *everyone!* He is the best president for people *everywhere!*

That is excellent! I said. And this, pointing to the flag on the same car, purple and white, reading NDP—this is his party?

He was really losing patience with me now. *Of course* that is his party!

I could see why the political operative in Pokigron thought it was a stupid question. On my drive from the capital I had seen hundreds and hundreds of these purple flags, but I had decided it was a cell phone company. It reminded me of the way Claro and other companies had plastered the countryside with flags and painted every building they could—with similarly bright colors—in the Dominican Republic and other Central and South American countries. The purple flags were everywhere. Even the poorest shacks of the Maroons, who barely had walls on their homes, had purple flags flying out front.

The Maroons trace their ancestry to slaves who escaped from the Dutch plantations, starting in the sixteenth century, and set up a number of independent tribes in the jungle, living alongside the Amerindians. They would occasionally raid the European settlements and free more slaves and take food and supplies.

I stopped at two different Maroon compounds—they don't live in houses so much as collections of buildings, mostly quite small, some of which are more or less verandas, just a roof, while others seemed like capsule hotel rooms in Japan, big enough for sleeping a couple people, and others seemed to be small storage sheds. The family groups were not nuclear, and some of the compounds were almost small villages, carved out of the jungle, built on the sand that was left after burning away tree stumps. In the first place I stopped, the women wouldn't let me take their pictures, although the youngest of the three would have said yes if she was alone. But they did let me take a picture of a kind of sitting room, with a thatched roof, several caned chairs, and a series of hanging baskets, everything—structure, furniture, household stuff—made by hand out of the stuff of the jungle.

Since Bouterse had led Suriname against the Maroons during the civil war, I found it hard to understand why they would be supporting his party now by flying his flags. The Maroons I spoke to had very little English, but they also seemed distinctly uninterested in discussing it with a stranger. On absolutely no evidence beyond that, I began to suspect that it was easier to agree to have the flag planted in front of their house than to refuse, that it was not enthusiasm for the cause but caution.

I asked Marianne about Dési Bouterse. Yes, she said. He is doing okay so far.

Some of the people out in the country love him, I said.

They *adore* him.

You sound less sure.

We have to keep an eye on him. You know, he has the past, she said, and looked to see if I understood. You have heard of the murders of December? That is the reason my family left the country.

Why you went to Europe?

Yes, my father was politician, I come from politician life. And my father was against the military government, like the murder people. That is why we left our country.

Because he was in danger.

Yes, because he was afraid. He felt we had to leave to live, and so we left.

Do the Maroons like him, Bouterse? I asked. Marianne was mostly Indonesian, with a mix of all the other races, she had told me.

The Maroons live better out near the rivers, she said, because they hunt and fish. It is better life for them than in Parbo.

But wasn't he the one that fought them in the civil war?

Yes, but already most Maroons are young, more are born since the war is over than before, and many lived far from the fighting. It is not important for everyone.

What about race? There doesn't seem to be racial tension in Parbo, I said.

Yes, no racial, but!—and she stuck her index finger in the air—politics is racial. They like the racial.

I was surprised to see the Chinese, even way out in the jungle, still owned all the stores. Do people resent them?

Well, no, she said. But we think: okay, enough. You own enough now.

Enough?

Yes, they own many business, now, okay, no problem, but enough. They don't put money in bank, no pay taxes, they help each other—if this business has trouble, the Chinese they give them money, help them. And—then—they move to the U.S., take money with them. Oh, yes! Suriname one stop, final stop, U.S.! Not good for Suriname.

And so now there is another election, will Bouterse win again?

You know, I don't like racial, but it is better if he wins.

I looked confused, so she explained.

Nobody knows how much money is in budget—better he gets elected, because then people will see—is there money there? Or did politicians take it?

Why couldn't a new president just say what the state of the budget is?

If new government comes in, and there is no money, people blame them. This way, Bouterse is elected again, and if people see he was lying, they go in the street, and whoosh, he is gone!

And that would be good?

You see! she said. Really, you understand. Immigrants get jobs right away, because they have school, they know things, they have the paper.

I somehow couldn't tell her that I didn't understand, that I didn't follow what she was saying—what does kicking Bouterse out have to do with educated immigrants? Since she had just complimented my understanding it somehow would feel rude to tell her otherwise, so I let it go.

And really we need people in government, she said, who are intelligent and have school, not just people who take the job and the money and know nothing. This is what we need.

That night I asked Jordan, my waitress at the tapas place, the same questions. She spent her first few years in a small town deep in the Amazon on the Brazilian border, her father a nurse, her mother a teacher, the only way in or out by small plane. She came to Parbo when she was school age. Her four grandparents were all born in Suriname, all mixed, except one grandfather who was Chinese. I am a quarter Chinese, part Indonesia, part Hindi—you know, Indian—but part other Indian, from here too, part, you know the N word, Negro—

Black, I suggested, African—

Yes black, she said, and part Jewish.

Part Jewish, I said. I went to see Jodensavanne yesterday!

Jodensavanne was a group of Jewish plantations, about thirty or thirty-five miles upstream from the capital, settled by Sephardic Jews, the majority from Portugal, who were slave-owning plantation owners. The first major synagogue in the New World was built at Jodensavanne in 1685. It was destroyed in a slave revolt in 1832 and never rebuilt. Nobody lives there now.

I have been there! she said. But I had a completely traumatic experience there.

I expected some horrible story of anti-Semitism. Instead, it turned out, she was struck by lightning. She still has marks on an arm and a leg, she said. She was unconscious for two hours, woke up blind, and remained completely blind for a number of hours more. That story—me expecting race tension, she offering a personal, natural disaster—was a common occurrence in Suriname. The Chinese grocery store owners all reported that they had no trouble. They like us, one owner said. They know they get fair price, I stay in business, I get for them whatever they want. This young woman, a racial cocktail, made with dashes of this and that, who spoke seven languages, and who seemed to have no commitments or complaints—she had grown up using the word "Negro" to say black, she knew that Americans and Europeans didn't like the word; it wasn't that she was ashamed or anything, she just couldn't remember the word we preferred.

Still, it didn't all add up. I had stopped at a memorial to the Maroons killed in the civil war of the 1980s. I had read reports of anti-Chinese and anti-Brazilian riots in Albina, the small mess of a town on the river border with French Guiana, and in the mining towns in the interior, and Marianne had been ready to describe the Chinese as a problem when pushed a little. But Jordan was a full generation younger, and when I asked her whether Bouterse was a good president, she shrugged.

I am not political, she said.

My guy in Pokigron—with the president's picture on his nice car and the flags on the roof and a belly full of beer at noon—was, I assume, some kind of ward boss, and his job was to tell everyone what a great president Bouterse was.

In the interior, I didn't hear any different. In Parbo, the one person I found who spoke against him—Marianne—hoped he would get reelected. I assume he will be. He cannot leave the country or the Dutch will have him extradited to face his felony charges.

In the meantime, the young people I talked to, like Jordan, were more interested in American culture, even Alvin and the Chipmunks, than local politics, all born well after the December murders. They do not seem to have an opinion one way or the other. For now, they are not political.

FRENCH SOUTH AMERICA
Cayenne-Kourou, French Guiana

The first hint I had that I was in France was the attitude of the night clerk at my hotel. Only two flights a week run from Suriname to Cayenne, and they arrive at 3:00 AM when they are on time, which they never are. When I got through customs and out of the airport there was not a cab in sight. It was 4:30. I asked the airport police to help me call a cab, a request they at first seemed to find odd, though it must happen twice a week. Eventually, they called one for me, and a half hour later it arrived. Forty-five minutes later, now true dawn, I arrived in front of the picturesque Hotel des Palmistes, on a palm-lined square with a view of the sea, the wooden hotel looking like something pulled from New Orleans's French Quarter and dropped here, on the edge of the South American jungle.

There was a pole across the stairs, but I stepped over it and went in. I woke the night clerk, who told me in French to go away and went back to sleep on his padded bench. I told him in French that I had a reservation. He shrugged, pointed to the computer, which was turned off, and said I had to wait for the owner.

When is the owner coming?

Soon, he said, and closed his eyes again. I went out and strolled around the square and came back. The clerk was sleeping. A housekeeper had arrived and was working, but no one else. I asked her if the owner had arrived. She said no, and I asked when she would arrive.

152

Je ne sais pas, she said, and shrugged.

I woke the clerk and said, look, showing him on my phone, I have a reservation, here is where it says I already paid. Just give me a key and let me go to sleep. Here's my passport. I've been up for twenty-four hours. He looked at me and said the owner is coming, and closed his eyes.

When?

Je ne sais pas. He flipped over to turn his back to me and went back to sleep.

I wrote a note to the owner, in English, saying she should cancel my reservation and credit my card, and that I would be back to check. I then walked up the street to find another hotel.

French Guiana is not a territory or protectorate or colony, it is part of France, a French *départmente*. The currency is the euro, the official language is French, the French air force, army, navy, and marines all have units stationed there, the police are part of the French gendarmerie, people vote in French elections, are citizens of France. Most of the people, however, are not of French ancestry, or at least not entirely. Some 60 percent of the population is mixed race, less than 15 percent European, 10 percent Amerindian, 7 or 8 percent African, about the same Asian. The country is almost identical to Suriname in many ways and seems to share only its language and service ethic with France.

Nothing about French Guiana, though, is more disconcerting than Kourou. The home of Centre Spatial Guyanais, Kourou is the European space center, where all European satellites are launched. There are three such space stations in the world—the others are in Florida and Kazakhstan. Just as no place in the world is quite as untouched by modernity as the southern border of the Guyanas on the edge of the Amazon basin, so nowhere quite screams the future like the Kourou launch site.

At the gate of the space center, an Ariane 5 rocket stands as a piece of sculpture. There is a small museum, but to enter the rest of the launch site requires high-level security clearance. A Soyuz rocket was scheduled to launch while I was there, but I couldn't join the spectators inside the compound. I drove down to the beach and watched with the local people. We saw the rocket emerge from the trees and then disappear into the clouds. It was sending up two Galileo satellites, one Chinese, one Italian, both for cell phones.

A few miles south, the unheimlich postmodernity melts away into the jungle, disappearing altogether when the road transportation stops, and river traffic begins, when the road literally drops into the river, and longboats take you where you need to go.

Before it was a space town, Kourou was a prison town. Starting in the middle of the nineteenth century, Guiana was France's Australia, and Kourou housed the worst of the worst of France's convicted criminals, most famously on Devil's Island. Tens of thousands of prisoners arrived at Devil's Island—including Alfred Dreyfus—and very few ever left. By the time the prisons were closed in 1947, some eighty thousand prisoners had died, and fewer than ten thousand managed to live through their sentences and were released.

It took some time to find a catamaran to take me to the islands, about two hours out to sea. The ocean was manageable but rough the day I went, and sitting on the foredeck meant holding on tight and plenty of spray. The three Îles du Salut—Île du Diable, Île Royale, and Île Saint-Joseph—no longer house prisoners. Île Royale has a dock, a restaurant, and a museum. The rest is a park, except for one hill that has infrared tracking equipment for the space center, since the rockets head over the island when they take off. Île du Diable, very close by, is off-limits; the currents around it are notoriously perilous, and little is left of the original stone buildings. Monkeys and agoutis—large rodents that look like gargantuan guinea pigs—have the run of the place.

When I got back to the mainland, I drove back along the coast to Cayenne and picked up a hitchhiker. She was a teacher, around fifty, and she had hitched to Kourou to visit her sister. She was now coming home. She was of mixed ancestry, she told me, mostly Maroon, but also Indian, French, Asian.

So do you think of yourself as Maroon? I asked.

Yes, she said, I suppose. Or mulatta.

And this is important.

Of course, I suppose, she said.

But you are French?

Of course! she said. Of course I am French! This is France!

Route D6 splits off from the highway south of Cayenne and quickly leaves town life behind. The whole country only has 250,000 people, as in Suriname 90 percent living on the coast. That means that only twenty-five thousand people live in the rest of the country. It is as if half the crowd at Yankee Stadium was scattered across an area roughly the size of South Korea, with its fifty million souls. A quarter of a Rose Bowl crowd spread over thirty thousand square miles. I drove down a narrow oil-and-stone lane for sixty miles, and the only people I saw were in a truck I passed; they were heading to the same riverhead where I was to catch a boat. The only other signs of civilization were a radio tower and a sign reading "Camp Caimans" about halfway. On both sides of the road, undistinguished rainforest, neither old nor particularly young growth, fully canopied.

The road ends, as roads do in the Guyanas, at the river, and my boat was waiting. A thirty-foot-long, five-foot-wide canoe powered by an outboard motor, it zoomed up the quiet Kaw River, rousing the jacanas—which flutter up noisily, flashing their chestnut, black, and white feathers, and just as quickly land back in the marsh—and occasionally a magnificent egret or heron. The sky was gray with roiling rainclouds, the wetlands wide. My boatman was a Lokono Indian of few words, but he slowed and pointed out birds, including the enormous hoatzin, or stinkbird, with its tufted head feathers and strikingly blue face, a cross between a feather duster and a pterodactyl. Two hours or so later we reached our goal, which was a floating hotel, a floating hostel, really, a handmade, three-story houseboat.

I had rented a hammock on the second floor. The amenities included a rowboat that I took on long excursions. A mile or so upriver, I found a herd of cattle, with Brahmin humps and horns, submerged up to the middle of their heads, munching on the marsh grass. They looked at me without fear or curiosity, and I assumed that whoever herds them does so in a boat. I just looked like another rancher. There were several cattle farms along the river, five or ten miles apart, the pasture all wetland, the animals living mostly below the waterline, the only road within fifty miles the one I came in on.

I had rowed upriver, and on the way back, as a light rain began to fall, I pulled the oars in and my hood up and lay back to let the current bring me home in the perfect quiet, broken only by the occasional rustle or cry of a bird or the sound of wind in the tall marsh grass. A black caiman, almost as long as my boat, idled upriver past me, ferociously prehistoric. I told the boatman, who turned out to also be the keeper of the hotel and the cook, about seeing the caiman.

Yes, he said. I know him. He comes by every day around this time. Sometimes I jump off the roof and do a cannonball next to him. He hates that. Now when he sees me on the roof he dives to escape me. We are old friends.

Do you like living on the river? I asked.

Yes, he said. The city is too crazy for me.

He had a teardrop tattoo under his right eye. He had other tattoos on his arms and neck and legs, but I asked him about the teardrop.

It's personal, he said.

In the U.S. people often memorialize their dead with a tattoo of a teardrop, I said.

It's personal, he said.

At night, he took me out in the motor launch with a flashlight and found some baby caimans that he plucked from the reeds and passed to me to hold.

One day they will grow up and you can cannonball near them, I said.

Yes, he said. We will recognize each other.

AMATEUR ELECTORAL POLLING
Pigeon Island–Georgetown, Guyana

Coming in from the airport was hair-raising. My driver had seemed friendly when he accosted me at the airport, and talkative, so I went with him. He didn't have a cab, it turned out, but a small bus, the size of a hotel hospitality shuttle. I got in the front seat and regretted it. The road was two lanes most of the way, with no shoulders, more like a backcountry road than the major artery between a capital and its international airport. It was after 9:00 PM and dark, and people were walking along the edge, a few bike riders, potholes full of recent rain, the ground muddy, and the vehicle clearly top-heavy with less than optimal shocks. The driver looked to be about fifty, voluble as I said, jumpy, and he passed other vehicles at will, whether it was advisable or not, and it came to me that he, like some 45 percent of the population, was Indian, and that this was one reason why people agree it is crazy to drive at night in India. It wasn't that smart here, either.

He had also overcharged me; the guidebooks and the woman at customs all said twenty-five dollars to town, but he insisted at the airport that it was thirty-five dollars because my hotel was far from the city center. It seemed possible. I had booked online, and sometimes "walking distance" to downtown can mean several miles. My hotel was in a neighborhood called Pigeon Island. I pleaded with the other milling drivers to tell me whether it was a fair price. They did unto their neighbor and shrugged.

We had a great conversation on the way in. He loved Guyana, which he and everyone I met agreed was a beautiful country. His great-grandfather had come as an indentured servant and worked in the cane fields. His grandfather and father had worked in the cane fields. He did too, but had risen to the rank of overseer and at one point had 104 people for whom he was responsible. But it was too much, all that responsibility. He was much happier driving a cab, he said, it was much more relaxing. For him, I thought, not his passenger.

I had read that there were racial tensions between Indians and blacks, and I asked if he thought that was true. He said, no, only politicians. Real people don't care, only politicians. One people, one nation, one destiny! he said, which is Guyana's E Pluribus Unum. He said it like he meant it.

These politicians now, he said, hooking his thumb over his shoulder, we throw them out. The elections were in May, just a month away. The elections, he thought, would change everything.

Since he felt bad about overcharging me, perhaps, or perhaps because he was irrepressibly sociable, he made a detour and gave me a little tour of the city. He had been pointing out the sites along the way—this is Chinese! he said. Biggest chicken farm in Guyana. This is army! This, school! This is Chinese! Cement! This plywood! Chinese!

I said it seemed that there was a lot of Chinese investment, and he said yes. I asked whether he thought this was a good thing, and he seemed not to have ever wondered. He pursed his lips a moment and then said, Yes! This!—he added, pointing, back to his tour—army!

Downtown Georgetown was quiet, the way Latin American cities are where you shouldn't walk around at night. None of the buildings were lit, the streets barely. There weren't many sites, but he valiantly pointed. City Hall! he said. Brewery! Clock Tower! Three minutes later we were at my hotel, a couple miles at most out the Caribbean coast.

The next morning I took the minibus into town for twenty-five cents and spent the day walking. The city reminded me of the Ninth Ward or Treme: wooden houses and buildings in serious disrepair, the sun hot and wet, most of the people black, the rest brown. I saw one group of three or four white people in matching yellow T-shirts with the name of their ministry in blue, and that was all.

Everyone was casually friendly. Even getting on the minibus, some would say, before sitting down, Good morning to all! If you met someone's eye, they said hello more often than not. Financial transactions were pleasant. People smiled and answered a gaze and a friendly nod with a smile and a friendly nod. Waiters said, I hope you enjoy, right? looked you in the eye and smiled.

The city has some large wooden churches (the largest wooden building in the world is St. George's Cathedral, I was told a couple times, although it clearly isn't true), some great shuttered colonial buildings, trash in the gutters, some open drainage, street markets spilling out from a few hubs, a Hindu temple, and a mosque here and there. There were halal signs and Indian spice and clothes stores, ayurvedic doctors—but it felt in some ways more like an African city than a South American or Indian one, except for the occasional dreadlocked men reminding me I was on the Caribbean.

I was taking some photos of the gingerbread Supreme Court building when two black men in their sixties asked me where I was from. I said Los Angeles, which didn't register right away, but then one said, Ah, America! I asked if I could snap some pictures, and they agreed. I took some together, some close-ups of each, and then showed them.

Technology! the same man said. The other, the sidekick, was an active listener but didn't speak a word. I asked if they were from Georgetown, and they both nodded.

It is beautiful country, Guyana, the speaker said. Only politicians make it bad.

Like everywhere, I said in solidarity. But you are having elections soon? You will have a new president?

Yes, this one is very bad, very much corruption.

And there is a lot of poverty, I said.

Nah, poverty, he said, but they both shook their heads.

What, no poverty? I said. They looked poor to me. The speaker was holding a piece of broken plexiglass, purpose unguessable.

Yes, of course, poverty, he said. But less than before. More economics now.

Their eyes were red, whether from ganga or illness I couldn't tell. They were sober in temperament. They were definitely interested in serious conversation, both engaged. We talked about the economy for a while.

Schoolchildren were walking by, school had let out, the kids and teens all wearing one uniform or another—tan with men's ties on both boys and girls, or green checked skirts for the girls, green slacks for the boys—and they walked in mixed-race groups.

Is there racial trouble in the country? I asked. The standard line was that in 1955 a split along racial lines in the original revolutionary party, the PPP, the People's Progressive Party—Afro-Guyanese against Indo-Guyanese—was the origin of the racialized politics of the country. The president whose term was ending was an Indian, Donald Ramotar, as was his predecessor, Bharrat Jagdeo, and their party, which kept the name PPP, was seen as the Indian party.

No! That is just politicians, he said. The Indians are more people than the black man—

Meaning a larger population, I said. Right?

Yah, them just slightly more, but enough for to all vote one way, they win, understand me?—but the "me" was mostly silent, like *understan'm?*

Yes, got it.

So the Indian politician, to get they votes, they make the people see problems, the racial, he said. But, no, the Indian—he waved his arms, to say Indians anywhere—You ask him, he like the black man. He like the black man fine.

And the same for you?

Yea! No difference. One nation, one people, one destiny, Guyana. Only for politics they make the trouble. You see, he said, meaning I would see, in time. The Guyanan are good people. There is—and it took me a while to get what he said next because it sounded like *Betty debt*—petty theft, but only that. You could slip in a street, nobody do nothing but help you. Good people, one people. Except the drugs, the alcohol, like anywhere. And this is very rich country! Many resource! Gold, bauxite, lumber, food, oil, like we talk—very rich country, only politicians, they take it all for theyself.

But you will throw them out, I said.

Yesah! he said, and his sidekick smiled too. We throw them out!

A cabbie the next day said: Who said that? A Negro? I had told him about the people telling me there was no race problem in Guyana.

An Indian, I said. Some black men too, but an Indian, and mixed people. One nation, I said, one people. I couldn't remember the one destiny.

Pha! he said. Of course it is racial!—he was Hindu and a PPP supporter, and a large, pear-shaped man, sturdy. The Negro, he said, he makes it racial! He puts the racial right in your face!

So there will be an election soon, I said.

Yes, next month.

What will happen?

Well, we don't know, of course! he said, and laughed.

What do you think?

I think we need to keep this government. We let *them* have it for a while. Yes! he said off my look, the Negro! We let them have the country and they bankrupted it, they ruined everything. This is why Guyana is so bad now. We need to keep this government, or it will be again disaster. Like you—you have Obama there, right? You don't want *him* again, do you?

I liked him a lot better than Bush, I said.

He thought about this. He wasn't ready to agree or disagree. He dropped it.

Why would you change this government? he asked, rhetorically, meaning the Ramotar government. We have good growth, we have good economy, good investment. We change, that all goes away.

But what do you think the future holds? I asked. Do you think there is a way forward, or will there always be racial animosity?

Well, we don't know, he said. Just keep this government for now, he said, mostly to himself. Just keep this government.

Late that afternoon there was a rally for the government and the PPP in Kitty Square in the capital and a rally for the opposition, the newly combined APNU and AFC (A Party for National Unity and Alliance for Change) in Berbice. I took a gypsy cab to Kitty Square, driven by a Jamaican, and I asked him if he was APNU, and he said, Nah, mon, comfort! I looked at him. Comfort! he repeated. Don't be midstream changing! Money good—don't get me wrong, plenty can be better, them crime, them government corrupt, but no, you don't change when things are good! You change when bad is comin'!

They say it is all racial politics, I said. But not for you.

Everything be racial, mon! But we all brodda and sistah, he said. For real!

The party secretary entertained the crowd with a description of the merger of the two opposition parties, the new coalition, and he spun what was basically a long conceit, making fun of them for being a couple, for being engaged, for having an unnatural sexual relationship—all a bit bawdy, unquestionably homophobic. Eventually he brought up the PNC, the People's National Congress, and started making threesome jokes. The PNC—the history is convoluted, full of splinterings and mergers—was opposition candidate David Granger's party before APNU, but it is apparently so tarnished by its own past abuses that it is best, from their side, not to mention it; they were widely seen as having committed electoral fraud in all the elections from 1968 through 1985, and there were murders involved. Each of the speakers referred to what they called the Granger Danger.

The party secretary came on and fired everyone up. We will destroy them! he said at one point. We will put the last nails in their coffin! And we will bury them! When one of the speakers was done, a band would kick in onstage, and the crowd would break into dance. A young black man with several other black men in PPP T-shirts grabbed me around the neck and started dancing with me, joyous. Two-thirds of the people were dancing, the others waving PPP flags and placards, drums and bass and keys and sexy women dancing and singing on stage, the crowd orgiastic. When the next speaker started, we laughed and fist-bumped, and I asked if he and his young friend were PPP. PPP! Yes! Of course! they said, and laughed, like, *what the*

fuck? Doesn't it look like it? but good-naturedly, and they motioned that
I should take their picture. They mugged for the camera when I did,
part rap star, part goofball.

I turned back to hear the next speech. It was the candidate for
prime minister, the one speaker who didn't have the oratorical
oomph of the pros. She managed to drop the temperature considerably. The people who lived around the square were hanging out their
windows and crowded onto their balconies with friends and families. On one balcony, amid a group of Indians, an extremely white-
skinned blond woman stood, and at first she didn't look natural,
like maybe she was a manikin, and it was, I noticed, the balcony of a
clothes store. But then she moved, and I wondered—huh! Is that what
I look like? Freakish.

Then Bharrat Jagdeo came on and the crowd went nuts, as if it were
Bill Clinton taking the stage. He gave a rousing speech—people say
he is actually still the power, the Putin to Ramotar's Medvedev—in
which he said to great cheers, flag-waving, and drumming, that the
APNU candidate for president is a liar, and, with the crowd frenzied,
said: Granger has put a potential prime minister comforter (an infant
pacifier) in the mouth of Moses Magamootoo (the opposition candidate for PM) and while Magamootoo is sucking on that comforter,
he has forgotten every principle he ever stood for before he made
this unholy partnership. But he said, still building, they both, David
Granger and Magamootoo, have such greed for power that they can
think of nothing else. They cannot think of education. They cannot
think of the private sector. They cannot think about the past abuses
of their party. They cannot think of Guyana.

This was followed, as it was meant to be, by pandemonium.

The crowd was probably 70 percent Indian, but each of the
speakers touted a completely postracial line. On my left, a stout,
solid woman of fifty or sixty said, when I asked if she was PPP, Yes!
They—meaning the PNC, I realized—almost killed my son! She had to
shout this in my ear because the loudspeakers were ferocious, a set
of drummers near us, there to sweeten the crowd response, flashed
after every one of Jagdeo's lines, and people engaged in a fair amount
of shouted-out call and response. It is a miracle he is still alive! she

yelled. I will support PPP until I die! She looked to be of mixed ancestry, or maybe Portuguese. We held each other's gaze for a while, until she saw something in my eyes and smiled; she had made her point, she was done.

The man on my right, also just passing middle age, said he had not made his mind up yet. He came to hear the speeches, he told me, and then he would decide. He had wanted to hear what they planned to do with another term, but he was not hearing it.

They say what a danger the others are, and how good they have made the economy, he said. Well, all the economies in the world are better, is this their doing? And they don't say what they will do next.

Yes, lots of negative campaigning, I said. I've been reading in the papers about corruption charges, murder charges, everything.

Yes, but not about their plans. You saw Suriname, right? he said, because I had told him I'd just been there. Why are we not more like Suriname? We are a richer country, but the people are poorer. Will they fix that? That's what I want to hear.

He had worked for many years in the mines in the interior. The crowd erupted in dancing and cheers as Jagdeo finished and the band started up again.

This could be such a beautiful country, he said.

The next morning I had a chat with an Afro-Guyanese man in the Rosebud Café downtown, a big warehouse room with great local food. I asked him where he stood on the election.

I hope for the best! he said.

And what would be the best?

Ah, for that, Time Will Tell, as Jimmy Cliff sings!

We talked about the rallies of the other day. He had the *Kaieteur News*, which leans toward the opposition. I asked about racial politics.

Yes, he said. Black and Indian, but not enough for one to win without the buying votes. This is what APNU and AFC say, that we come together, we leave race behind, and we have to come together. But who can tell? You look this—and he held up his paper, pointing at pictures from each of the two rallies—they look the same, so who is bringing more people together? He gave me a beat, then answered himself: Jimmy Cliff! he said, and smiled.

The PPP rally had quite a few black people, I said, as well as Indians, but not everyone there was PPP. One man came to hear the speeches and was disappointed. Nobody had a real plan, he told me, no program.

Exactly! he said. They at each other, but nobody say, *this is what we do!* He handed me the paper, pointing to an op-ed inside, where an ex-PPP member from the countryside complained that none of the promises PPP made in the 2011 campaign had been realized. They need to tell the people the truth! the man said.

The APNU has its own problems with the truth, I said. I read about the election fraud and violence.

Yes, but you know they say, we need to leave the past where it lay and talk about the *future.* Otherwise, we relay back to race war. We need to look forward.

You sound like you're leaning APNU, I said.

No, I'm not leanin'! he said. I'm just quotin' the man. I just want them to do good government and let the man *be.* But I'm not leanin'! If you lean, he said, winking, you like to fall!

ZONA DE TOLERENCIA

Bogota, Colombia

Bogota is a stretched-out city, a city of neighborhoods, some leafy
and almost suburban, some industrial, some slummy, some anonymous rows of brick condo, some hillside shantytowns, some old and
cobblestoned, some burnt-out and still decaying. The grid curves and
winds and makes no sense to a walker, and the socioeconomic slice
changes so frequently that it is easy to wander but hard to find anything. Calle 17 can be sometimes north, sometimes south of Calle 12,
and Avenida 17 can be as much as a mile west, or sometimes slightly
east of Avenida 1. So when I wanted to get to La Candelaria, the old
colonial center, I needed to navigate and renavigate from my hotel,
up north of the Zona Rosa. The Zona Rosa, which has the reputation
of being the city's hip spot, its nightlife center, is itself, during the
day, hard to bring into focus—some coffee shops, yes, some clubs
maybe, but it peters out in every direction and seems to have no
center.

As usual, I kept my map in my pocket and as much as possible
just roamed. I figured I would just stick close to Avenida Carrera 15
because my hotel was near the corner of it and Calle 102, and it would
send me south through the length of the city. It disappeared now and
then, and I'd find 14 or 16 and follow them for a while. I walked all
day, through neighborhood after neighborhood, some vaguely interesting, mostly not. I stopped and had lunch and walked some more,
snapping pictures, mostly of the graffiti. As the sun got low, and it

was about time to take a cab back—I didn't know how many miles I had managed, but quite a few—I found myself in an industrial wasteland, with no cabs going by and no place for dinner, nothing. I walked in the direction of what traffic there was and eventually the city began to thicken again. It seemed to be a run-down neighborhood, but there were cabs on their way in—all full, a good sign.

Coming around a corner, I found myself on a very lively street with dusk approaching. I had been pulling my camera out and snapping pictures every once in a while, but this was the kind of neighborhood where a 35mm camera with a hefty lens would attract the wrong kind of attention, so I didn't reach for it. A young woman came up behind me and tapped me on the shoulder. She was heavily made-up and had on the minimal amount of fabric a person could wear in public. She smiled and pointed to my pack. I looked and saw that the last time I had returned the camera, I hadn't zipped it up, and it was hanging open. She wagged her finger at me, meaning *bad idea!* and walked on. I thanked her and zipped up, and shifted the pack in front of me. I always tell myself that it isn't that expensive a camera, but for a street thief on the poor side of town, it would be a hell of a score.

Cabs were pulling up and groups of three and four young men were hopping out, laughing and smoking, and maybe already a bit lit, and the further into the neighborhood I got, the more obvious it was that I had landed in the Zona de Tolerencia, which, as it sounds, is a place where everything is tolerated—it is the center of prostitution in the city. The block I was on was lined with brothels, young and youngish women leaning out of doorways beckoning. I stopped and talked to a few, and apologized for my lack of interest in their services. They were unconcerned; the night was very young, and they did not seem in the slightest bit worried about filling up their dance cards. That made it easy to chat while they were waiting for the night to begin. Yes, they said, this is the Zona, although it is also called Santa Fe. The economy was good, they agreed, but not good enough, and this barrio, one said, *¡Qué asco de sitio!*—What a dump! Bogota is better than before, they agreed, but still, not good enough. I asked if I could snap their pictures, and they said sure but pulled me inside the door to do it, and then made sure that my camera was put away before I went back outside. They agreed I should be careful and not flash such things around.

When I stepped back outside, it was full dark. A taxi pulled up to the curb disgorging four drunk young men with cigars, slapping each other on the back, and I hopped into their cab before they closed the back door. I gave the cabby my hotel's address, and he said, English?

Si, pero puedo hablar el Español, I said, and we chatted half in Spanish and half in English the rest of the way.

You are here alone? he asked.

Yes.

Here? He adjusted his rearview mirror so he could see me, and shook his head.

Yes, it is dangerous, this barrio, I guess?

For a gringo, yes! he said, with a disbelieving laugh, meaning *duh!*

Yes, I said. The women told me.

No, I mean dangerous, really dangerous. You are crazy.

People were nice, I said.

People are not nice! You know last week, a German, he is kidnapped in Santa Fe, and they chain him to a radiator in an abandoned building and beat him until he gives them his PIN code. Then every day, they go to the ATM and take out the maximum until the card is empty, and he is starving and no bathroom. Then they throw him out the window. Eight stories. He is dead on top of a car.

Ay! I said.

Yes, he said, looking at me again in the mirror—he can't believe what a numbskull I am and wants to retain a picture in his mind of the stupidest American he had ever seen. Another man, he went on, they just keep him in the back of the bordello and make him charge to his credit card, fifteen thousand euro, then they kill him. The putas, they just say, we know nothing, we don't use that room, we don't know, he is just dead! And that is that. The police, they do nothing, they get paid by the killers.

We talked a bit about other things, his kids, politics, his neighborhood. Then he looked at me in the mirror again and shook his head.

I guess that wasn't smart, I said. It was still daylight when I got there.

Puro loco, he said, shaking his head. Truly crazy.

As I got out of the cab he said, you seem like a nice guy. Don't be such an idiot. He smiled and waved as he drove off into the night, quite possibly to get more passengers on their way to Santa Fe.

AFRICA

BAKSHEESH 101
Tangier, Morocco

I was new to North Africa, and as it has been for many Americans, Morocco was my first venture beyond Europe and North America. I had come across on the ferry from Algeciras, just a day before, driving a miniscule Peugeot rental I had picked up in Paris. I'd had to replace the driver's door window in Granada, after the local drug addicts had done a quick sweep through the car as I slept in a shabby hotel in the old city. I came across the Straits of Gibraltar on a big rusty ferry and sat at the bar drinking shots of espresso and shots of brandy, feeling like an adventurer, watching the coast of Africa approach.

As the ferry docked, I leaned over the rail and watched a crew member jump onto the pier, drop a massive loop of foot-thick rope around an mammoth cast iron cleat, which was his job, and then hurriedly hop down behind a wall, which was not part of his job, and begin to pull cartons of cigarettes from his overalls, dozens and dozens of cartons, Gauloises and Marlboros, in a well-oiled smuggling routine. A man was there to pick them up in a wheelbarrow. The crewman felt eyes and looked up to see me. He smiled and shrugged; I gave him a small salute and started down to my car.

The border, I had been warned, was a place where such law bending, including bribery, was endemic, so I should be on the lookout for scams and should be prepared to pay a little baksheesh. My guidebook said ten dollars would solve most problems. Sure enough, as I drove off the boat and came around the first corner, the immigration and customs station just in sight at the end of the quay, a couple of men flagged me down, waving official-looking papers. I rolled down the window, and it was starting to occur to me, looking more closely, that these guys might be completely freelance, not officials at all. They said I needed to give them my passport and sign in, handing me a clipboard.

Who are you?

We are the officials. Passport, please.

Ah, I said. No. I tried to give them their clipboard back.

No, sir, passport, the man with the thicker moustache said.

He wouldn't take the clipboard. I started inching forward, holding out the clipboard. Eventually, he grabbed it, said something—I assume a version of "fuck you"—and I drove forward. I'm not sure what their play was going to be; I left them yelling at me and approached the next phalanx of guys, who looked more convincingly official—they had not just clipboards but plastic-encased photo IDs hanging from their necks on lanyards. They carried leather cases full of forms.

I drove up to one, who handed me a form, which I filled out and handed back to him. Passport, he said, and fifty dollars.

Is that for a visa? I asked. I thought I didn't need one.

No, for my *chef*, he said.

That seemed nutty to me, so I watched the action, and saw that these guys were walking the papers up to a couple different offices. I got out of my car and barged past my facilitator to the actual office, where a fat, uniformed immigration agent looked up at me briefly, and then back down at his papers. I tried to hand him my passport and he ignored me.

My passport, I said.

Without looking up he pointed back at the intermediary, who had followed me.

This was my first bribery-financed border, and I had no idea how to navigate it. But the guidebook had said ten dollars was the magic number. I turned to my nonofficial, a bit defeated, a bit defiant, and handed him my passport and ten dollars. He looked at the ten dollars with deep disappointment.

This will not be enough, he said.

Try, I said.

I was drawing on my inner Humphrey Bogart, acting like I knew what I was doing. It was too late, though, since I had already proven to this guy that I didn't have a clue. He took the money and passport and disappeared.

I watched the rest of the border at work, and everyone was using one of the lanyard ID guys. There was no way to know how much they were paying.

Did I just screw myself? I wondered. Was the guy out selling my passport?

He came back twenty minutes later. He held my papers, not offering them to me. He was in his thirties, in Western clothes.

Baksheesh, he said. You need to give me. For my *chef*.

That ten dollars was for your *chef*, I said.

For me, then, he said.

I don't know why, but I gave him another ten dollars.

Merci, he said. And now, for my *chef*, he added, holding out his hand.

He wasn't in the slightest abashed, nothing in his demeanor suggesting, look, I know I'm asking for extra, but please. There was no new entreaty or urgency in his voice, no sign that the two ten-dollar bills had registered—he looked exactly as imploring and distressed as he did before. Yes, I said. Ten dollars for you, ten dollars for your chef. Now I go.

He looked at me for a minute and entered phase two of his routine. For my *chef*! he said again, hand out, indignation mounting.

I held out my hand.

My passport, I said. Again, I'm not sure why, but he handed it to me. I walked back to my car, and he followed me.

A little baksheesh, he said. For me. He wasn't angry anymore.

I thought, what if the guidebook is out of date, and I'm being an asshole?

Didn't I already give you too much? I said. I should have given ten, and I gave, twenty—did I give too much?

He looked at me, sneered slightly, held out his hand, and said, for me, for my *chef*.

SADDAM HUSSEIN AND THE POSTCARD SALESMEN
El-Djem, Tunisia

The Roman Coliseum at El-Djem, three hours or so south of Tunis, is maybe more impressive than the one in Rome, but that might be just because it isn't in Rome. It is almost as big, and it's in Africa. Like all such monuments, it has its share of gewgaw hawkers, T-shirt salesmen, tchotchke vendors, and touts, and as soon as I got out of my car, I was surrounded by boys shouting for my attention—English! Deutsch! Italiano!—all with the same wares, pushing their postcards, refrigerator magnets, scale models of the coliseum, and coins in my face.

It was 1991, and the first Gulf war had just started.

A relaxed, handsome forty-five-year-old man with dark curls of hair, smoking a cigarette, saw me surrounded and confidentially summoned me over. He was holding the same collection of stuff and looked like an Arab Marcello Mastroianni. Not for the first time, I thought about what a thin strip of water separates Sicily and Tunisia—closer than Key West and Cuba, closer than Dublin and Liverpool. He pursed his lips and shook his head slightly, then repeated the summoning gesture, smiling, meaning, *don't worry, they will find other customers, come talk to me.*

You are American, he said, when I came over, trailing the shouting and shoving boys.

Yes, I said. How could you tell?

He yelled at the boys and made an aggressive shoulder move toward them. They scattered. But you are not from Virginia, he says. Most Americans here are from Virginia.

No, I'm not from Virginia, I said, confused. Later, in Tunis, another man asked if I was from Virginia, and it occurred to me—Yasser Arafat still had his PLO headquarters in Tunis at that point, and most Americans in the country were probably from the CIA.

Tell me, he said. Why does George Bush hate Saddam Hussein?

Many people are asking this question, I said. I apologize for my government.

He waved his hand, as if to say, *this is not about sentiment.*

Saddam Hussein is not the problem, he said. The fundamentalists, they are the problem. They are the ones who want the world to bow to their will. They are crazy, and like all religious warriors, they will stop at nothing, because, of course, they have god on their side. The U.S. should worry about them, not Saddam Hussein. And so I ask, he said, finishing up, why does George Bush worry about Saddam Hussein?

It occurred to me that we were also right across the water from the birthplace of the Socratic method. One of the boys continued to push his collection of postcards toward me, standing behind me and thrusting them toward my hand, glancing fearfully at my interlocutor, who, without taking his eyes off me, sidled over when the kid wasn't looking and gave him a tough smack on the back of the head.

They say, I began, that it's because of the invasion of Kuwait—

Nonsense, he said, calmly. If the U.S. wanted to stop Hussein at the Kuwaiti border, they could do that—easy! Look how they destroyed his army in just a few days. If they wanted to make him stop?—very easy. They make him stop. So why?

He clearly already had his answer, and so I said, well, why?

Because Bush is the oil business, my friend! Because he wants Saddam should play nicer with the oil business! This is a message, not from the U.S., but from the oil business! But, he said, holding up a finger, this is very dangerous game, very dangerous.

While he was saying this, another boy had snaked his way around to my side, wordlessly imploring me to buy something. While still talking, still confidentially giving me his view as a North African realist, the Arab Marcello slowly reached around behind me and held the last inch of his cigarette to the side of the boy's neck. I heard the flesh sizzle. The boy screamed, slapped his neck and ran away, cursing the man.

I apologize for this, Marcello said. These boys, they have no parents, and I am a father figure to them. But as I say, this is a dangerous game the Americans play, because without Saddam, Iraq is a problem. Kurds in the north, they would blow up the country tomorrow. The poor Shi'ite masses, they wait for deliverance. The Sunni elite, they will fight to the death, like any aristocracy, until the guillotine takes them all. No, Saddam is very good for peace. Saddam is good for us.

The boy, back with the others at a safe distance, held his neck, wincing and throwing looks of pure hate at Marcello.

Here, Marcello said. Buy these postcards. I know you do not want them, but since the war, there are no tourists, and we need to eat.

I bought his big item, the accordion with twenty views of El Djem. I bought a couple souvenir pens. And a tchotchke.

I should buy from the boys too, I said.

No, please, he said. I will take care of them. They have shown me disrespect, and it would be bad for them to be rewarded for it.

CAMEL HERDERS

The Tunisian Desert

A hundred or so miles into the desert from El Djem, two young camel herders—one around nine, the other thirteen—were walking a dozen camels across the baked rocks. I stopped and took their pictures, and they were fascinated by me, by my car, by my camera. I was fascinated by them, their open faces dirty, sun-battered, living outside for how long at a time? Weeks? So far from any adult, from any people at all, responsible for ten or twelve nasty, unruly beasts—because camels can be really nasty, and they are ten times the size of these kids. This was no lemonade stand, no lawn-mowing job. The flat, scrubby desert stretched out to the horizon without a sign of human beings except the road that, in another fifty miles, would reach Qibili, the oldest town in Tunisia, inhabited long before humans domesticated the first camel. But camel herders have walked this desert for five thousand years, and for these boys, on many, many of their days, life was the same as it had been for millennia, except that a few times a day, when they happened to be close to the lone highway, a vehicle from the future would speed past.

They did not, like the kids in the towns, ask for *cadeaux* or *stilos*—or for dinars. But I saw the older one looking down at the passenger seat, where the accordion of postcards of the coliseum and my tchotchkes sat. I handed him the album, and he took it and started flipping through it, showing it to the kid who I guessed was his brother. They were rapt, and without another look at me they began

to wander away, automatically following their camels, the two of
them holding the unfolded set stretched between them, looking
at the images, and I realized: I had come five thousand miles to see
a monument two or three hours drive from where they wandered
every day, and they have never seen it. They might never see it. How
many miles do they cover in a day? Not enough to get to El Djem.
Where is home? They were already almost too far away to see clearly,
except that their heads were together over photo after photo as they
receded from the road, their camels in front of them. I continued to
watch until I could no longer tell camel from boy, a few specks. Then
the desert swallowed them, and was empty.

PYRAMIDS, MUSEUMS, SEWAGE

Cairo–Giza, Egypt

Arriving at the Cairo airport with an Avis reservation is a lot like arriving without a reservation. I had booked a car online for $150 a week, and the man at the Avis counter wrote me up a ticket for twice that and a little, $320. I showed him the expedia.com printout.

Oh yes, he said. That is the price in the U.S.

I said, no, you see, this is the price for a car here in Egypt, see? Cairo airport Avis, Egypt, this price.

No, he said, that is the price for here in Egypt *in the U.S.* Here, he said, pointing at the contract he had just written, is the price for Egypt in Egypt.

Luckily, I had been to Morocco and Tunisia already, and so I knew that bargaining meant staying relaxed, staying calm, not being in a hurry, cordially moving the checkers around the board. Unfortunately, it was already 1 AM when I arrived, bleary, from LAX, and he was the only auto rental agent left in the building. He knew that.

Hmm, I said, this is no good. Too much.

He was trying to hand me the contract to sign, and I was pretending he wasn't.

Where is the taxi stand? I asked, and he pointed lazily over his shoulder, a *not my problem* gesture.

An hour later, I was on the road at a rate of three hundred dollars. What a negotiator!

At that hour the roads were fairly empty, which makes driving a little easier—a lot easier, I would realize once I experienced midday Cairo traffic, among the craziest in the world. But what I hadn't counted on was the thoroughness with which colonialism had been reversed, so that not a single sign, anywhere, was transliterated, much less translated, unlike my *Rough Guide* maps, which were in English only. I did not know a single letter in Arabic. Somehow I managed to traverse the city and get onto what I assumed was the road to Giza, Pyramid Road, heading west. There were many hotels and discos along the side of the road, which made sense, given what the *Rough Guide* was saying, and I was relieved to see them, but none of them had very much in the way of signage, either. I knew the hotel I had booked for the night was one and a half miles east of the pyramids—so I figured, easy, I would drive all the way to the monuments, then backtrack the one and a half miles, and bingo, bed by 5 AM. Eventually, I came to a gate across the road, with several heavily armed guards and a small guard shack.

I got out of my car as they fingered their trigger guards and looked at me warily.

The pyramids, I said, and I pointed down the road, past the gate. How far?

They looked at each other, gave me nothing.

The pyramids, I said, making an upside-down V with my hands. Then, making a gesture like turning the page of a book, or like jumping over a fence, eyebrows raised, asking if the pyramids were over the gate, beyond the gate.

They were watching.

How far? I asked again, put my palms together, then pulled them apart horizontally, shrugging.

They looked past the gate, then back to me, and nodded, yes, and said, El Ahramat, and pointed, yes they were over there.

Okay, great, I said. One kilometer? Holding up one finger.

They nodded, and pointed to the ground.

Two kilometers? I said, holding up two fingers, thinking, I should have learned a few words beyond *salaam alaikum*.

They rolled their eyes, and one pointed a finger back, over his right shoulder.

Ahramat, they said.

Ahramat? I asked.

Pyramid, one said.

Yes, this is the gate, I said, as if more English would help. Beyond the gate, three kilometros? I asked—no idea why I used Spanish—but this was one question too far. They were very much attuned with each other, these two, and they came to the end of their rope at the same time. They moved toward me, and I again saw their guns, which I had forgotten about. They waved me back, frowning. *We're done playing now*, the gesture said, *go away*.

I got back in my car and figured, okay, my hotel is somewhere between zero and one and a half miles from here, and there is nothing for the first half mile, so I basically have less than a mile to check. I'll just hit each place until I find it.

The next morning, after roughly an hour's sleep, I woke to the sound of Cairo traffic: a million metallic geese in a frenzy. Egyptians use their horns to announce that they are changing lanes, to announce that they are done changing lanes, to announce that they are about to pass, that they are passing, that they have finished passing, and each person being passed, or in the general vicinity of the lane change, responds to the honks with acknowledging honks in kind. Experienced Cairene drivers claim that they can close their eyes and drive perfectly safely, and I have to admit, once I got used to it, I understood how the constant bleeps were helpful—they marshal another sense in the service of movement, and after a while, my ears could actually see the traffic. When I got to the relative quiet of Israel, I missed it.

But that morning, the flock had descended way too early. I stuck my head under the pillow for a while, but then, as was inevitable, capitulated. I ate breakfast, got back in my car, and entered the swarm of honking machines, driving the mile and a half to the Pyramids. That put me precisely at the spot where the gate crosses the road, the spot where I had encountered the guards.

It was then I realized: the men I had interrogated only hours before were practically leaning on the Pyramids. When one had pointed his finger back over his shoulder and said *ahramat*, he was almost touching one of the smaller ones. Right here, they were saying. The Pyramids are right here.

The Cairo Museum, or, officially, the Museum of Egyptian Antiquities in Cairo, was the saddest museum in the world. Enormous, its many rooms are overstuffed with stones and statues and relics and junk, not all organized: carvings from two thousand years ago leaned against the walls, with other pieces from three thousand and four thousand years ago leaning against them, sometimes piled three and four deep. Some seem to have fallen over and broken. Some parts of it looked like any museum, with sarcophagi lined up neatly in rows and mummies in glass cases, but much of the place felt more like a storage garage than a museum, and nothing looked very clean.

Legends were scarce. The Rosetta Stone had some explanatory information that did not include, as I remember, the fact that it was a copy of the actual Rosetta Stone rightly or wrongly housed in the British Museum.

In one flat-topped glass case, ancient coins were laid in rough, augured depressions in an unfinished board, made when, in the 1860s? No telling, but it looked like it was made with hand tools. Several coins were missing, with only their drilled ghosts to tell their size and shape. What legends there were had been scotch-taped below each coin at some point, and from the brittle yellowness of the tape it looked like the 1950s. Several had fallen off and lay, slightly curled, some upside down, in the dust at the bottom of the case.

As I walked away from the museum after a long day, dodging the insane traffic, a hot wind came up suddenly and whipped a spray of liquid into my face and shirt. Smelling it as I wiped it off, its source was unmistakable. Roaring through the culverts under the street, the gust had splashed raw sewage up through the vents in a manhole cover—I saw it happen again, now at a safe distance, with the next blast of desert air. I wondered how many years this had been happening, and if the locals knew to steer clear, or if somewhere in the sewer system, a door was suddenly missing or a manhole cover stolen, something that had helped turn the sewage system into a wind tunnel.

This may, I realize now, have colored my memory of the museum. Both nineteenth-century institutions—museums of antiquity, city sewage—were falling to pieces in Cairo, as if getting ready to be overtaken, once again, by the desert sands. Only the endless, ungovernable rush of cars and trucks insisted that it was at the turn of the twenty-first century. Coming through the traffic, a police wagon, built fifty years earlier, with wooden sides and small barred windows at the top, was apparently part of one of Mubarak's round-ups of Islamists. A dozen hands were thrust out of the windows, many holding Korans. I could see only their arms and hear them yelling. They were arrested, but they were not cowed. I thought how they must be baking, so many jammed into that space under the Nile sun.

I went in search of water.

SANDSTORM IN THE SINAI, DUST STORM IN THE DELTA

East of Suez–Nile Delta, Egypt

On my paper map of the Sinai there are a series of small billows,
like the clouds Pigpen trails in the Charlie Brown comics, running
north to south, twenty or thirty miles east of Suez. I checked the
legend and was surprised to see that they represented sandstorms.
It was the first time I'd ever seen that in a map legend, and it hadn't
occurred to me that sandstorms could be localized like that, though
it made sense. I thought of the high wind corridors in California—
along the Grapevine above San Bernardino, for instance—or the hur-
ricane coast in the Gulf. I wondered whether there was a season, like
there is for the Santa Anas or for typhoons.

Driving from Cairo across the Sinai from the Suez Canal, the world
is already fantastical. The ships, coming through the canal, when
seen from the highway a mile away, seem to float through the sands,
nothing but sand in front of the enormous tanker, nothing on either
side of it but sand. The enormous things slowly move through the
desert like a special effects version of a dream, like a minimalist,
silent version of a Chris Nolan movie.

It didn't come as an entire surprise, then, when the air grew thick.
I checked the map. Sure enough. Here we were, in a sandstorm.

Did this mean the sand was always blowing here? Is this like fog
in San Francisco, something you just learned to drive through? I
watched a couple trucks barge into it and followed them. But it was

worse than I'd thought and getting thicker. I pulled over to consider. To wait or go? I had an image of a dune growing right where I sat and wondered how long would it take to bury me. It was accumulating on the road surface like snow before getting whisked this way and that by the wind. Sit and wait, or plow ahead? Which was the greater risk?

A couple of trucks barreled past me. They must know what they're doing, I thought again, they do this for a living, and followed. I'd driven in Malaysian monsoon rains, in New England blizzards, and if the truckers could do it, so could I. I drove on, hoping to see a truck's taillights ahead, but couldn't. Every once in a while a huge gust cleared the road enough that I could see that I was still, almost, in my lane. Then it grew too thick, and I could see nothing. I drove until I felt my right wheels hit softer sand, on the shoulder, and quickly yanked left. If I went off the road, I realized, there was no going back, I'd start sinking into the sand as my wheels spun. If I stopped on the road I'd be crushed by the next barreling semi.

I slipped and slid, trying to keep my wheels on the macadam, and managed, at ten miles an hour, in a panic of whiteness, to feel solid road under all four tires. Like a snowstorm, the sand would accumulate unevenly, and I'd hit a thicker patch and be floating, driving by feel to react if I hit either shoulder, peering into a solid tan wall of opaque, swirling sand, getting darker as I drove, my wheels slipping more.

Driving blind stops time, like spinning out of control, and all vigilance becomes a combination of denying and awaiting death.

It was a dozen miles, all told, and of course, I didn't die. Eventually, the sand became thinner, a semi screamed past me laying on its horn, and then I was back in the Sinai sun.

I didn't take a lesson from it that was particularly usable. When sailing, a squall can come up, and it can kill you. It's no reason to stay on land.

The fast road to Alexandria from Cairo flies across the desert just east of the Nile Delta, a road that, like most highways in Egypt, provides constant images of the distribution of wealth. I watched an expensively groomed guy in a white shirt and tie, with a cigar in his mouth, driving a large black S-Class Mercedes sedan—a car that costs more than a hundred thousand dollars—pass at about a hundred miles an hour, a heavy-duty dump truck going fifty miles an hour and being used as a personnel carrier with what looked like sixty or seventy sun-beaten laborers standing up shoulder to shoulder in the back, with a few hanging off the sides and a few more sitting on the roof of the cab. The desert here is ugly, with roadside attractions ("The Lion Village!"), like the drab outskirts of many cities. The road is close enough to the delta to see irrigated fields and some clumps of trees.

Alexandria itself is crumbling into the sea, as if it wants to join its library. The Corniche, the promenade along the water—which people walked to, dodging ten lanes of screaming traffic, one lane at a time—is decked out in concrete knobs and flourishes, painted white at some time, but now flaking into the sand, gaping cracks everywhere. At the edge of the city impromptu dumps pile trash for dogs to sift through. The run-down Cecil Hotel still has its guest book on display, reminder of grander times—Somerset Maugham, Cole Porter—but sits in insignificance as the city with each new day becomes more overstuffed with rural migrants.

Along the back roads of the delta returning to Cairo, there was a different kind of richness and deprivation, a canopy of palms for miles, water flowing to fields, but everywhere dust, dust, and more dust. Clouds of fine dirt swirled in the air, stirred up by each passing car, truck, and donkey cart. It would hit the palm frond canopy and circle back to the ground. So many people walking, riding bikes, driving animals and rickshaws and motorbikes—all sending more dust into the air—that it seemed impossible that people could breathe. And teeming! So many people! It seemed impossible, too, that millions had left to swell the two cities. The ground was thick with people.

For more than fifty miles, I saw nothing clearly. And yet the image of the humming delta, I knew from the start, would never leave me. The place, as overwhelming as the sandstorm, as disturbing as urban poverty, as thrilling as the Sphinx, sits somewhere in memory that is not quite an image, not quite an idea, not quite a feeling, something powerful and unfocused. Ancient, unfathomable, unseen, churning. Marco Polo despaired of telling half of what he saw on his travels. That estimate seems high.

PRETTY PICTURES
Stone Town, Zanzibar

The photographs make the place irresistible. Palm trees, white sand, the hefty sailing dhows with their triangular gray sails. The resort brochures could be for Tahiti, with thatched-roof hotel bars and infinity pools and fruit-bedecked drinks. Even the *Lonely Planet* guide, which like the rest of the series tries to avoid any Club Med–like commerciality, has almost the same shots. Tropical beach paradise.

I'm guessing the resorts live up to it, but I didn't go to any. I took a ferry across from Dar es Salaam and along the way gave myself over to the romance of the endless parade of homemade-looking sailboats of every size, all with the characteristic lateen sail, a puffed out isosceles right triangle, the long side of which is wrapped around an upper boom that soars on a forty-five-degree angle, half again as high as the mast, the lower end sticking out in front of the bow. The origins of the sail are lost back in the ancient Persian Gulf or Red Sea, and they no longer ply the Mediterranean as they did for millennia. But along the coast of Africa they are more common than any other kind of sail. The boats look as old as the gods, and straight out of an adventure novel.

Approaching Stone Town, the romance starts to subside, the ramshackle place looking slightly less picturesque by the minute. Besides tourism, Zanzibar's economy runs on spices and raffia, and despite how that may sound, it is no more exotic than any crop farming, and in the equatorial heat—the island lay on the same latitude as the

Congo and the Amazon—hauling and grinding up the raffia palm leaves for rope is as dusty and torrid and drudgeful as any work on earth. The people in Stone Town are at work, and tourists, as far as they know, are rich people who get driven through town fast or, more often, land at the airport and never come through. Tourists mean nothing, unless a niece or nephew lands a resort job.

There are a few old Portuguese buildings, and there are the toiling poor. And somewhere, miles down the coast, there is tropical beach paradise. I spent a few hours walking around the sun-blind town and was hit by a powerful desire to leave.

It is unpredictable, I find, when the misery in the world will turn from an object of study and compassion into a sense of defeat and futility.

I couldn't meet an eye to start a conversation. I lost all sense of mission, of purpose.

I gave in to the despair and walked back to the ferry dock.

AIDS AND OTHER MALADIES

Morija, Lesotho

Lesotho looks like its geological history. Thrust out of the African plains, it is the only country in the world that lives entirely above a thousand meters in elevation; 90 percent of the country is more than a mile high. Approaching from the east, you see the Drakensberg Escarpment sticking straight up out of low-lying grasslands more than three thousand meters (ten thousand feet), forming the entire border of Lesotho with South Africa's KawZulu-Natal Province. There is a pass, but only navigable by four-wheel drive, and only on good days.

The plains of South Africa stretch on for many Montanas in every direction, slow-rolling, big-sky stretches of wheat and pasture, with the old-school metal windmills of the American West, the same cattle grazing, the same small towns with a feed store, a general store, a church, and a few houses. In the middle of it all, up pops quiet, mountainous Lesotho, a kingdom of sheep, cattle, and goat herders. Almost the entire population is engaged in agriculture, and yet they manage to grow less than half of the food they eat; the rest is delivered from international aid agencies. The people live in the same woolen blankets, the same small round, thatch-roofed, yurtlike stone homes, and the same Dr. Seuss conical hats that they had hundreds and hundreds of years ago.

South African farm country completely surrounds the kingdom—Lesotho is not only landlocked, it is South Africa–locked—and that land is dominated by the Boers; many of the little towns are predominately white. Crossing the border into Lesotho means returning to black Africa, but of an unusual kind: Africa with cowboys.

Driving into the country below the capital, Maseru, I felt I had entered a strange new realm, with the shepherds in conical straw hats that narrowed to a point two and a half feet over their heads, and cowboys that looked like Argentinian gauchos with a thick woolen blanket over a shoulder, as sartorial as it is functional, and with a long coiled bullwhip in one hand, reins in the other. I asked one for a picture, and he consented. As I was snapping it, feeling I was catching the remnant of a little-known and almost lost civilization, his cell phone rang. I have one picture of him without it, and then a dozen with him on the phone.

Up in the mountains I ran into a Swiss doctor, a volunteer with Médecins Sans Frontières, working in a small clinic. He said that some 40 percent of Lesothos's women in the prime of their lives are HIV positive, and since people only visit doctors when they are otherwise out of hope, more than 90 percent of his patients had AIDS.

He was walking in the small town of Morija, the Swiss doctor, with his two adorable young blond children, two and five, and his charming but stressed wife. The doctor looked like he was twenty-five, although he must have been thirty; his wife looked even younger. She was a doctor as well. I asked how long they had been in Lesotho, and he said six months.

How long will you stay? I asked.

I don't know. People do burn out, he said, because it is hard to face the odds. And of course it is not the most fun place to live in all the world!

His wife smiled wanly but said nothing.

There is no movie, no restaurant, nothing, he said. We know this, but sometimes—

His wife half-smiled again. The children were hanging from the rails of a fence, talking to each other in French. He told me about the very minimal equipment and medicine they had available, about the way every patient was a double patient—obstetrics and AIDS, broken bones and AIDS, tuberculosis and AIDS, heart disease and AIDS.

While we were talking a man approached, wearing what looked like bits of military uniforms, a hat resembling one from the U.S. Civil War, various pieces of rope and what were perhaps improvised medals of honor hanging from his shirt. He carried a broomstick like a rifle over his shoulder. He was declaiming—I heard him before I saw him—what sounded like Bible verses, something in biblical cadence. I couldn't tell the language, although some words were distinctly English. As he got closer, the children stopped chatting and stood up straight.

Money! he said, quite clearly. Then he launched back into his rhythmic oratory.

Not today, Mgembe, the doctor said.

Money! he said, this time angrily.

Should I? I asked.

Please, no. Not today, Mgembe, money tomorrow.

He seethed and seemed about to do something but stopped, perhaps only because he couldn't decide just what he wanted to do. He looked at me.

Money! he said.

I said, following the doctor's lead, Tomorrow, Mgembe. Money tomorrow.

You know Mgembe? he asked.

Yes, the doctor said. We all know Mgembe, but now we are talking, okay? he said, pointing to me and himself and his wife. We talk now. Mgembe tomorrow.

Mgembe looked at each of us, launched into his oracular monologue again, and marched away.

What language was that? I asked.

It isn't, he said. He speaks in tongues, I suppose you would say. He is schizophrenic, and, well, we aren't sure what the problem is, there is some trauma too. We have such irregular access to drugs, and of course, patient compliance is hopeless, and so we have no way of gauging if anything we have tried might have had any chance to work. People like Mgembe are the ones we can do least for, really— when the body needs attention we can do many things, but the mind—there is no institution in this country, there is no place for people like him to go.

He scares the children, his wife said. They know he is unpredictable, and it scares them.

Yes, the doctor said. We live like the Sotho in many ways, and the children adapt fine—to the quietness of life, to the tragedy even, to the flies and heat and cold and deprivation. But they know this man is sick in a way that is different. The mentally ill—even the children know we are at a loss, that these poor people are lost. It makes them very nervous.

We said goodbye, and I drove up into the far mountains, to the end of the road, and spent the night at a small place owned by a white man formerly from Zimbabwe, staffed by locals. It is empty country, nothing but rock faces and a bit of snow. Every twenty miles or so a tiny village appears with a dozen of the classic Sotho round, thatch-roofed houses. It is hard to see how even a goat could scrape a living off the endless rocks.

As I drove back, I picked up two people hitchhiking, a young man and a woman I took to be his wife. They got into the backseat.

She was fevered, shaking, sweating and shivering under several of the heavy woolen blankets. He was on the verge of tears and wouldn't take his eyes off her. They spoke no English. I drove them, three hours, to the hospital in the capital.

UNDER A TREE IN THE DISTANCE
West of Moamba, Mozambique

Driving into Mozambique from Kruger National Park in South Africa, the bush disappears. The landscape flattens and there is nothing. The riot of wildlife vanishes, nothing grows more than a few inches off the ground. Twenty or thirty miles in, I saw a lone tree several hundred yards away, and it had drawn a human family to it.

They had erected a makeshift shelter. There was a dog, and there were several small children, a few pieces of dull clothing hanging. In all my travels I have never seen a more obvious image of rural poverty and isolation. They were far enough from the road that I couldn't make out facial features, and they probably couldn't see into my car. I didn't have the heart to go talk to them. I've always regretted it.

Two minutes later, they had been dissolved by the desert, the tree vanished, nothing but rocky stubble in every direction. I drove on toward Maputo, with no sign of human beings but the thin two-lane blacktop.

ECSTASY IN MAPUTO
Maputo, Mozambique

Walking into my hotel in Maputo, I was surprised to see, sitting around the lobby, a dozen women in matching bright yellow gingham dresses—imagine a Steven Spielberg film about—no, I have no idea what the film would be about, but it had something of his art direction, too much, really, too on the nose, too iconic, too colorful, too perfect. They had heavy, peculiar makeup on, white—not whiteface exactly, but odd as fuck, thick patterns of white all over their faces, like ghost paint. The dresses were more like women dressed for the set of *Hee Haw* or a community theater version of *Carousel* than anything African, flouncy skirts and lacey white trim at all the edges. They all looked unhappy.

I said hello to several of them, who glanced at me like I was vermin, while the rest ignored me. The sheer incongruity of the otherworldly getups, which seemed to scream for attention, and their apparent disdain for the attention it elicited, prompted me to ask if a picture was possible. They looked to their leader, who was a bit older and heavier than the rest, and she shrugged, so I took pictures. They looked at the camera and frowned. All of them. The white makeup, the angry look—and they all had it—was a commitment. It drew you in even as it repelled. I asked at the front desk, and it turned out they were a group of traditional singers, performing that afternoon downtown.

They were one of a dozen acts at a festival sponsored by the French cultural center on the edge of a small city park. Some groups performed inside in a big theater with mics and amps and banks of speakers, some outside on a short concrete stage with a roof held up by four columns, a very informal setting with no amplification, and a variety of mismatched chairs and tables strewn around for the audience. The women from the hotel performed there; they sang—fourteen women in all—almost entirely in unison, in a very high, hectoring register, with a percussion ensemble of four men accompanying. It was easy to feel that whatever was traditional about this was alive, not calcified, not museumified, but real, not much changed over the last century or so, but vital. The songs were loosely choreographed—or better, they were constructed with a series of tightly choreographed moves that the leader switched in and out of seemingly at her improvisatory will, and the rest followed with precision. The rhythms were what one might expect—African with touch of Portuguese, complex, funky, exciting—and the dances involved a lot of dropping to the knees and stretching backward until their heads were almost touching the ground, with an alternating series of shimmying and jerking movements back and forth, arms out, all in strict formation. At times a vocal soloist would start a line, always in an extremely high near-screech, to have it echoed by the group. They never, ever smiled, and it was mesmerizing. Something about it was a response to slavery and colonization—those ridiculous Western dresses, with frilly trim, the essence of missionary enforcement, and the white paste on their faces, and the anger in the performance, all of it fully owned by these women; it was as if they were saying, you missionaries will never, ever get these dresses back, these are now ours, and ours alone, like our despair and our grief at the centuries that will never return.

At the concert, a young, hip, light-skinned black man asked where I was from, in what I learned was the accent of Durban, South Africa. Come join us, he said. His friends included two kids from Mozambique, and a guy on a business trip from Italy. They had all, more or less, just met. They said that if I liked music, I needed to come that night to a bar, very close to my hotel, to hear one of the best local groups. The band would start around 11:00 PM. I thanked them. It might happen, it might not, we would see. I had a long talk with the kid from Durban, who was very smart and cosmopolitan, about the various subcultures in South Africa.

If you want to see what South Africa could become, he said, you should come to Durban.

I had just driven across great swaths of the country, and we talked about each of the places I had been. Yes, the racist plains. Yes, cosmopolitan Cape Town.

But you know what we say, he said. Cape Town—that is not South Africa, that is Europe. And it can't be the future.

Why not? I asked.

The whole country can't become Cape Town because it would take too much money. But Durban is like Cape Town without the money. Durban is the future for us.

I asked him and his new friends what they thought of the group we had just watched.

'S a trip, the Durban kid said.

I loved it! the guy from Italy said.

What is it? I asked

The alpha of the local duo said, I don't really know. Traditional, but from the north, we don't see it here.

No idea, said the other. My first time seeing such a thing.

A number of other groups were performing around town, several at a large stage nearby. We all walked over, but in the darkness of the theater—there were regular theater seats, but no assigned seating—we got separated. I made my way up to a balcony so I could watch the crowd as well as the bands. The first band had a professorial young man as the leader on acoustic guitar, with a flute player and rhythm section. They played very clever, cerebral music in an alt-pop vein, and the crowd was very enthusiastic. The young man seemed to be a local hero.

When they were done, a big funk band set up, and when they started, the place exploded. The band was like James Brown and Prince and Papa Wemba had started a supergroup. I had been talking to a sybaritic trio of indeterminate but obvious sexuality, two women, thirty and forty, and a very pretty guy of eighteen, and when the music started they jumped up and danced in funky, hardcore expressions of bodily joy, and I did the same, in my own less elegant and virtuosic way. Strobe lights came off the stage, adding to the trippy feel. I was moved, and watching them I was inspired to dance in ways I had never managed before. The trio was doing serious fake-fucking, doing comic fake-fucking, doing serious funk, doing parodies of their own best moves, swinging from laughter to intense, almost masturbatory concentration, and managing to find balance in the most extreme positions, like hip-hop dancers or Alvin Ailey or Pilobolus. But none of that quite gets it: I felt that I had never seen anyone really dance before.

On the way back to my hotel I dropped into the bar that the group of young people had mentioned. The guys from earlier in the evening cheered—they were all there, and I had somehow become their mascot—and the band was just starting. An alternative rock band with reggae flavors and some Afrobeat, they played in the middle of the tiny club, right on the floor. An interesting mix of young Maputo hipsters crowded around them, and the feeling was a cross between a club and a house party, one where the host never wants you to leave. I only wandered to my hotel as the darkness was starting to crack.

In the very late morning I made my way back downtown and heard a rumbling bass in the distance. I followed the sound for quite a while, past the edge of the recognizable city, and down into a ravine, where I could see a large building through the eucalyptus. As I found my way down, I could see it was a sports arena and could tell the music inside was loud. At the main door a woman handed me a small baggie with a teaspoon of what looked like yellow oil in it, tied off at the top. She ushered me inside with a smile. Thousands of people were on the floor and in the stadium seats, reaching up to the ceiling. A stage in the center held the band I had been hearing, bass, drums, keyboards, guitars, horns, and a large gospel choir, along with two women sitting in chairs. A man was praying into a microphone, but I couldn't see him; he was somewhere offstage.

I was ushered up to an empty seat fifty rows up. I was the only white person in the place, except the keyboard player, who was albino, but nobody seemed to care. The people I passed were welcoming enough, but absorbed by the drama down below. The preacher was on the floor, just to one side of the stage, and a line of supplicants was standing in front of him. He would put his head up to theirs, touching foreheads, and he would hold the mic up to their mouths and let them talk for a while, and then he would start talking not just to them, but to the room, praying and preaching. I couldn't understand a word of it, couldn't even tell what language it was, frankly, but it was easy to follow the emotional arc of each petition and response, which always ended with the entire church in boisterous, thrilled applause accompanied by swelling music—the music never stopped, it just sometimes got quieter—and when it swelled the choir kicked in for a few bars, joyous. The preacher went through this with a couple of people in that line, and then one of his helpers, far up in the stands, handed a wireless microphone to a person standing in one of several lines up in our top tier, and he made his case, and the preacher hopped up on the stage while the man was still talking and closed his eyes, and when the man stopped, he waited a long beat, and then, once again, he started talking quietly, then built it in volume and emotion, then built it, and built it, until the crowd wept and stomped and yelled hallelujah and applauded and the choir rejoiced. Then he hopped back down to the line waiting on the floor.

He kept this going for an hour or more, and for I don't know how many hours before I got there. After a particularly large emotional moment, he said something from the stage that made everyone hold out their little baggies of oil and gave a rousing blessing, and the choir sang its happiest hymn of the day, and people were transported, basking in religious ecstasy. It was hot and getting hotter. People were fanning themselves with whatever they had, but when the spirit got moving, they forgot everything and sang along with the choir.

The preacher was indefatigable. I never quite got who the two women were on the stage, both very light-skinned, both very pretty, one a little older than the other, it looked—his wives? A wife and daughter? They were undaunted and tireless too, sitting straight-backed for hours without a break, beatific, maybe, or maybe a little bored and superior? I couldn't quite read them. The choir, in robes, was sweating profusely but remained as energetic as when I walked in. The albino keyboard player was calm, in control, conducting the instruments and voices. The drummer and bass player chilled—I knew the type—they were enormous, heavy, solid, and they played their instruments with their hands while their bodies rested.

The preacher was hard to read too. He wasn't desperate, he didn't have that Elmer Gantry wound, he wasn't an over-the-top show-man, and he wasn't the classic breast-beating sinner. He seemed relaxed and perhaps even sincere, but he was running a fairly large business—he had a hundred people, at least, on his payroll that day. Perhaps he was an honest fee-for-services provider. Perhaps he was just beginning to be bored with his own act, and I was seeing a late-career version of it—maybe when he was younger he would have betrayed his own damage. Now he was impenetrable. When I left he was as much of an enigma as when I walked in.

I made my way back out into the painful heat of the day and started trudging the long way home, not entirely sure if I was going the right way. A cab honked from behind, and I turned, hailed it, and got in.

What are you doing here? the cabbie asked as I told him my hotel. I had made my way far from the center of town.

I heard music, I said, and just followed the sound until I found it.

Down here? he asked. Music?

Yes, back there, at that sports hall.

Music at the sports hall? At noontime?

Yes, I said, a church service, amazing.

Huh, a church service in the sports hall.

Yes, a famous preacher, apparently, He was on the stage, but there were people in the audience with microphones, and people would take the microphone and tell him some trouble, I think, and then he would say a prayer for them.

Huh, he said again, not very impressed.

It was quite a production, with a band, and a choir in robes, and they handed everyone little baggies of some special oil, which he blessed at some point—

Wait, he said, this was not Prophet Emmanuel Makandiwa, from Zimbabwe?

Yes, that's right, Makandiwa, his name was on the posters. He's from Zimbabwe?

Ah! My goodness! the cabbie said. Was that today? I wanted to go to that! Ah! Yes, Zimbabwe, he's a great healer.

It's still going on, I said. It's still full.

Ah, but it is too late, he said, too late. Ah, I wanted to go to that!

He was upset at himself and turned up his radio. Scratchy Nigerian pop.

After a minute he turned it back down.

What hotel? he asked.

THE TOURIST CORNER
Victoria Falls, Zimbabwe

The fifty-million-dollar bills are sold for an American dollar a piece to tourists. They are worth considerably less than a dollar as money. The former jewel of Africa—with the best school system, the most robust economy, the most vibrant contemporary culture scene—has been brought to its knees by the most corrupt and brutal regime on the continent, its careening decline overseen now, for the thirty-five years since independence, by Robert Mugabe.

Mugabe is no dope, though, and as much as he lets the rest of the country fall into chaos, he keeps Victoria Falls well patrolled and unbothered. One of his last sources of foreign currency is the tourism the Falls attract, and the people going to Hwange National Park and parks in the other Four Corners countries—Zambia, Namibia, and Botswana, all a quick hop from Vic Falls.

So the town, with its several blocks of lodges and hotels and souvenir shops, is fully policed. People in tourist-police uniforms wear bright vests to stay visible, and they are everywhere, a pair of them every half block in the tourist center. They make sure the hawkers don't pester the tourists too much and step in if they do, keeping an eye out for security issues of all kinds. The foreigners are insulated, living in their hotels, walking to view the truly sublime and fearsome falls, buying knickknacks, waiting for their safari tour to start, or waiting for their plane out.

I wandered off the grid, though, away from the center, and immediately I was picked up by a couple of salesmen, one selling scarves,
the other with a short stack of multimillion-dollar bills.

The scarf man was anxious, in his early thirties, I guessed, and
clearly in need, perhaps high. He had four scarves to sell and had
started the bidding ridiculously high, like he was new to the game
and following someone else's directions. The moneyseller was a
decade older and had the red eyelids and droopy, glassy eyes of the
hardcore alcoholic. He was pushier, and unlike the younger man,
whose desperation was outmaneuvering him, this man was at home
in it. He was scarier.

I showed the moneyseller that I had already bought some, holding
up a small packet of the same bills he had.

Buy some more, he said. There was no play in his tone.

And I bought a scarf like this red one, I said to the other man, just
this morning. It is back at my hotel.

Buy another one, the scary man said, learning.

We need to eat! the younger man blurted out.

We were in a bit of a gulley, where a walking path connected two
parts of town. I realized that I shouldn't have wandered down it,
even though it was bright midday.

Okay, I said, I will buy some more, but you will have to come with
me back to the hotel. My wallet is there, my money there.

The younger man was happy at this idea, the older knew every
dodge and blocked my way back up the path.

You are European and you walk with no money? I don't think so.

American, I said. I turned out my pockets to show him. Empty.

You have money belt, he said. You have wallet in shirt.

No, I said, and started to take off my belt. I had the slightly absurd
idea that it could serve to protect me.

Give me your shirt, the scary man said.

Look, I said, patting the pockets, and opening a couple buttons in
the front, No wallet.

Yes, give me your shirt, he said.

You want my shirt?

The younger man was shifting his weight from foot to foot, apprehensive, not happy with the way this was going either.

Follow me back to the hotel, I said, pushing around him, and I will get a shirt for you. You can't have this one.

Because there is money in it! he said, like he had caught me. He grabbed my arm as I tried to pass him, and the shot of adrenaline summoned a bit of theatrics.

Get your fucking hand off me! I said loudly, inches from his face, sticking my chin out. He smiled, held his hands up like a basketball player denying he had committed a foul, and I walked fast up the path. They followed me, trying to get in front of me again, haranguing me, until I got back to the business zone, where they stopped and let me go.

I turned to look at them. They were defeated, despondent. The tourist police had clearly quarantined them for breaking some rule or other. I picked up a couple rocks, reached into my back pocket and got some cash out, and placed a bit under each rock, eight feet or so apart, so they would each have to choose one, and the older guy couldn't bully his way to both. Then I went over to the tourist policewoman and stood past her, so her back was to the men, and asked her where my hotel was, though I knew. As she was telling me, the two men ran up, grabbed the cash, and returned to the valley of their banishment.

They counted the bills as they walked away. They didn't look back.

I kept walking until I hit the bridge to Zambia. The bridge is a playground for tourists, with a zip line across the river gorge and a bungee jump halfway across. The tourists jump off the bridge, freefalling for what must feel like forever but is only less than a minute.

POROUS BORDERS

Botswana

For a hundred miles and more as the crow flies, the border between northern Botswana and the Namibian panhandle follows the Linyanti River and then the Chobe River. The twists and turns mean the actual border is twice that long. The crossing from Chobe National Park into Namibia's Caprivi region requires a check-in at a riverside border station, a building the size of a barbershop, with a tin roof and mud walls.

The small boat from Botswana pulls up onto a patch of sand in front of the station, where a half-dozen people wait, some to be picked up, burdened with plastic bags and boxes of goods, some to meet a boat bringing people or supplies. The sun is hot, but there is a light breeze. A couple kids sit in the sand next to their mothers. One hard case wanders the beach, a man about fifty, the worse for wear, both his body and his clothes, substance-sick—why do borders attract such men? Do they like the idea that they might cross over, somewhere, somehow?

The border agent was a man of about forty-five, heavy-set, slightly bored.

How many of these border stations are there along the river? I asked him.

You only need one, he said. He kept a straight face.

Yes, I just wondered. There can't be that many, and so many miles.

Yes, he said, uninterested.

So people can cross wherever they want, can't they?

Well, yes, but they can only enter the country here.

Officially.

Yes, officially.

So if someone was smuggling ivory or rhinoceros tusk, they wouldn't come through here.

They would be arrested.

But they could cross just a half a mile from here, and you wouldn't know.

Of course, that is possible. But they cannot enter.

They could cross, from Namibia, into Botswana, then cross into Zimbabwe—

Why would they do this? he asked. They can enter straight into Zimbabwe at Kasane.

But if they are smuggling . . .

Yes, he said. But that is what they do, smugglers, they sneak around. We cannot stop people sneaking around. People will do this. But they cannot enter Botswana.

He stamped my passport and I officially entered Botswana. But I did not actually cross the border at the station. I got back on my boat, which took me some miles upriver to my camp. Elegant giraffes stood on one shore. On the other, upstream, elephants.

IN THE REEDS
Okavango Delta, Botswana

The dugout canoe was low, thin, and long, and I sat on a cushion in the middle, trailing both arms in the water, while Robert, standing in the back, slid us through the reeds with smooth pushes on a ten-foot pole. The delta is silent, save the noise of the bugs and birds, no machine noise, no highway for dozens of miles, no flights overhead.

The water was cool, the reeds thick on either side, and I felt encased. It was late afternoon, and the sun was low enough that the reeds made a tunnel of shade. Peace itself. We stopped to look at tiny frogs, the size of an aspirin tablet, each bright green and red and black and white. A heron flew quietly over. A most exciting peacefulness.

We slowed at what was a bit of a lagoon, a side eddy of the river, to see a family of hippos twenty yards away. Hippos are the real killers, responsible for many more deaths than lions. But these hippos seemed completely uninterested in the passing boat. I noticed that Robert, who was happy to stop and let us look at the tiny frogs and at a nesting bird, slowed but didn't stop for the hippos. No sense giving them ideas.

Farther downstream, the reeds closed in tight, and there was just room for us to get through. Up ahead I heard water rushing and assumed we were about to hit some faster water, some kind of rapids. The swishing and splashing got louder, and then Robert slowed us down. In front of us a herd of some forty elephants was crossing the stream, from old matriarchs to yearlings and younger, the largest able to walk along the bottom, the smaller needing to swim. They too were uninterested in us, and we were mere feet away, so that as they came out the other side, they towered above us. The babies seemed proud of making it across, the mothers slightly proud but not as impressed as me and the baby elephants were. Was I projecting? They were, undeniably, invigorated by the water and had a little bounce in their step as they wandered off. One young male came over toward us and snorted, neighed, and ran off.

CULL THE HUMANS

Hwange National Park, Zimbabwe

I flew in a small bush plane from Victoria Falls to a dirt landing strip inside western Zimbabwe's Hwange National Park and was driven to a tent camp a couple dozen miles south. On the edge of the Kalahari Desert, much of the park is extremely dry, the road mostly sand, the vegetation mostly short—mopane trees and desert brush.

The six-thousand-square-mile park was founded by Cecil Rhodes in the 1920s, I was told, as a hunting preserve, and right at the start waterholes were dug and pumps installed. The increased water would increase big game.

Now, almost a hundred years later, seventy manmade permanent watering holes, their diesel pumps chugging away, have completely transformed the ecosystem. In the evening, elephants come to water, and I did a rough count of some five hundred elephants of all ages coming for a drink at a single site. The country as a whole has an elephant population between two and three times the optimum suggested by leading conservation and wildlife groups, but in Hwange the problem is worse. Across the park, the devastation wreaked by the elephants is easy to see. In the mopane woodlands, the trees are reduced to shredded stubs. In the Kalahari woodland, major tree loss and erosion are visible everywhere. Biodiversity suffers as a result. Species disappear. There are as many as twenty times as many elephants per square mile than can be sustained without environmental damage. Fewer still would inhabit the park if the artificial waterholes stopped pumping.

The people who work in the park—rangers, guides, camp staff—have different explanations for why there are so many elephants, but the most common and most persuasive: tourists love pachyderms.

In the 1970s and 1980s, when the government allowed some elephant hunting as a way to cull the herds, they were not just concerned with the ecosystem. Elephants were overrunning farms, trampling humans, and chasing them out of their houses. When culling was halted in 1986 under international and tourist industry pressure, there were some twelve thousand elephants in Hwange. That number has now quadrupled and continues to grow.

The tent camp had a twelve-by-fifteen-foot pool for tourists to cool off, and in the evening the elephants come and drain it.

The other travelers in the camp, all Americans, refused to consider the question of culling. Cries of disgust and distress would silence the conversation, but I would bring it up whenever I got a chance—I know, perfect guy to have in your camp—and one day one of the guides, a tall, broad-shouldered man named William, said, perhaps we should cull the humans instead. This was greeted by applause from the Americans. I said, if we culled all the humans, nobody would feed diesel to the pumps, the water would stop, and 90 percent of the elephants would die. Again, cries of disgust and distress. Yes, William said to me, with a straight and unsentimental eye. Yes, it would solve all the problems.

In the great African night, listening to the elephants slurping up the pool water once again, I couldn't shake the sense that I was not in the wild at all, but in a New Jersey safari park, on a slightly larger scale, and less carefully managed.

The elephants, whatever the havoc they might be wreaking, are magnificent. Each one is magnificent. When hundreds of them gather at dusk at a single watering hole, throwing water in the air as the sun sets, they are majestic. I am a tourist. I love elephants.

EUROPE

DREAMING ARIZONA

Veliko Tarnovo, Bulgaria

Once called "The City of the Tsars," Veliko Tarnovo was the capital of the Second Bulgarian Empire—I know that most people haven't even heard of the first, much less the second, but in the thirteenth century, the second empire was the dominant power in the Balkans and included most of Greece, Albania, Serbia, Macedonia, and much of Romania and Moldova. Veliko Tarnovo was one of the cultural capitals of the Middle Ages. The empire was divided over the next century and then overrun by the Ottoman Empire. The city was further reduced to rubble by an earthquake in 1913.

Painstakingly rebuilt, it was the one Soviet-era concession to the idea of historical preservation in Bulgaria. After the collapse of the Eastern Bloc in 1989, historical reconstruction continued and has increased now as an active enticement to tourism. There are more bed and breakfasts than in most Bulgarian towns its size, and its churches and cathedrals are dressed up for visitors more than for congregants. It clutches its hillside like a town in Umbria or Languedoc, picturesque, although much of the local housing is considerably more rundown than in such places—it is still, after all, Bulgaria.

I found a place through one of the guidebooks and pulled in as the sun was setting. The proprietor's son greeted me in English. He had lived in Chicago for a dozen years, but he was now back home.

217

In Chicago, he told me, he worked in electronics sales and had married an American girl. They had a baby, and he had managed to buy a house. He had been illegal, having overstayed (by eleven years and nine months) a tourist visa, and so the house was bought in his wife's name, and he wasn't too worried about immigration. He was married, and if necessary would become a citizen. He was very happy.

The American dream! he said, with a scowl, pensive.

They started the process of legalizing his status. They hired an immigration lawyer to advise them, and part of the deal was that he needed to leave the United States to avoid prosecution for illegal entry. He was to fly back to Bulgaria, and then his wife could bring him in legally, as her husband, and he could start the road to citizenship.

Before his marriage, if he left the country, he would never have been able to return; his visa having been once abused, he would never get another. But marriage made it safe.

I was very happy to come home here, he said. After so long, it was beautiful—I had not seen my family, my mother, for twelve years, and so this was good opportunity. And as citizen, I could bring my mother to meet her grandchild or come back again with my family. I would be free to travel!

Then, I am back here one week, he said, and in mail comes divorce papers—he makes a slash in the air like Zorro—like that! She crosses me off the list of the green card.

He was heartbroken and miserable.

Why? I asked. Why did she do it?

Why, he said, why? She now owns house. Nice house. Three bedrooms. Why? Was she conman? I don't know. She don't talk to me. And I, I am in love with my daughter, who now lives in foreign country. I am depressed.

He spent two thousand dollars—this is a lot of money for us, he said—on a divorce lawyer, and the best the lawyer managed, in the way of custody, is a half-hour Skype call on Saturdays and a half-hour on Sundays.

Every way I think, he said, it breaks my heart.

He got his hopes up, during the election, hearing Obama talk about immigration, and he gets mad, he told me, when he hears the anti-immigration talk.

Arizona! he said. Does Arizona know me? They don't like poor Mexicans, nobody likes poor people, but I am rich! I am American Dream! I have job, own house!

Then he seemed to remember that he no longer owned a house and went silent for a minute.

I have an American daughter, he said.

PERESTROIKA IN THE BALTICS

Vilnius, Lithuania

The Baltic capitals—Tallinn, Riga, and Vilnius—are the last places one might think might house Soviet nostalgia. The New World Order has taken hold there with a vengeance, and the commercial bustle and the theme park–like dressing-up of historical landmarks give these cities a Vegas feel, complete with casinos and strip clubs parked amid the cathedrals and guild halls. But a cabdriver in Vilnius, driving a nicer cab than I had happened upon in St. Petersburg or Moscow, had nothing good to say about the postbreakup years. He noticed me looking at an old woman begging on a street corner, then pointed out that there was one on the street corner opposite as well. I had seen many beggars on the streets in this part of the world: amputated veterans with tin cups in Russia; threadbare babushkas in Odessa picking through dumpsters in clothes that looked like they might have been made in Stalin's time.

Perestroika! the stocky cabdriver spit out, with a mocking thumbs up. He hissed *Kapitalizmas!*, using the Lithuanian rather than Russian *kapitalizm*, throwing the car into gear before giving another vicious, satiric thumbs up. Old people!—once more with a scowl and his thumb stuck in the air obscenely. He turned in his seat to see my expression, which apparently was sympathetic enough for him to continue. He was a Russian, he told me, and wanted to know what I was. American, I said, and he repeated he was Russian but born in Lithuania, where he had lived all of his fifty-odd years.

He was a bit jowly already, had most of his hair, gone gray. Only 6 percent of the population of the country is Russian, but 15 percent of Vilnius is.

So perestroika is a bad thing, I asked.

Very bad, he let me know.

And it was better being part of CCCP?

Da. Yes, he said—shaking his head, and pointing at the begging women. No good now, he said. We pulled up to the bus station, and I paid him. He looked me in the eye.

Maybe capitalism, good, America, he said, his English not quite as primitive as my Russian, shaking his head and pointing to the ground. Here, bad.

Capitalism, I answered. Not always good for America, either.

I was minutes from getting on a bus for Latvia, and we had used up our language, and anyway, given the intractability of our world, perhaps there wasn't much more to say. He gave me the famous disgusted-yet-noncommittal Russian shrug and the slightest trace of a smile before resuming his scowl and getting back in his cab.

OLD ART NOUVEAU
Riga, Latvia

Sergei Eisenstein's father is everywhere in Riga. Street after street is filled with Art Deco apartment buildings from his architectural studio, all a bit baroque, each a different pastel with white trim, each unique and yet recognizable, ranging from quietly dramatic to the outlandish, with enormous women's heads in bas relief, bare-breasted women holding up victory wreaths flanking entryways. If they melted like Dalí's clocks, they would look like Gaudí buildings. They speak of a late Imperial European world I can only partially conjure.

His most famous buildings, on Alberta Street and Elizabetes Street, were built starting in 1903 and 1904 and 1905, when Sergei was seven, the year the first movie theater, the Nickelodeon in Pittsburgh, opened, to show one-reelers and shorts. Features only started to be shown after World War I, and a few years into that, Sergei's *Battleship Potemkin* was released, about a mutiny that took place twenty years earlier, in 1905, in an Imperial world that had by then, in Moscow, where Sergei worked, completely disappeared, while another was just coming into being.

IMMIGRANTS
Helsinki, Finland

Helsinki is a bite-size Scandinavian capital, full of well-trained musicians performing in the street, cosmopolitan in its design and restaurants and even its traditionalisms—the folk and classical music, the saunas, the midsummer celebrations, the wooden buildings—are all appreciated with a cosmopolitan air of connoisseurship. A simple, unaffected cosmopolitanism, they hope. The Finns like having an unassuming culture. Everything is pleasant and civilized. Their pride is quiet.

Some of the men looked like relatives of mine. My mother had a Finnish grandmother who I never met. She married her Finnish husband in the States. They and their daughter, my mother's mother, were all dead by the time I was born. My mother liked to claim Laplander blood, and I was never sure why. She had a slightly Central-Asiatic cast to her round face, so it is possible, and I suppose she liked the idea of being descended from reindeer herders, more romantic figures than the steady burghers of the Finnish towns. In either case, I knew I was supposed to feel something, "returning" to the ancestral land where my long-dead progenitors were born. I felt nothing.

My great-grandmother's was a heroic story: she shipped out barely a teenager, alone, coming to America in steerage, with no English, hoping to find her emigrant cousins in New England. Hearing the story as a kid, I tried to imagine the fear, the sense of displacement, and the extreme destitution necessary to lead her and her parents to think throwing her on a transatlantic boat, alone, at that age, to never see her again, was a good idea.

In front of Helsinki's main train station, waiting for the train to St. Petersburg, I spent some time talking to a seventeen-year-old immigrant from Somalia who had lived in Helsinki for some ten months. He was decked out in American-style hip-hop gear, a flashy sideways cap, gold chains, and bright oversized pants and jacket. He spoke some English and some Finnish, and bore no trace of Somali culture that I could detect. He appeared aimless in a cheerful way, with bright eyes, big energy, and an open face. I asked him some questions. Was he was in school? No. What kind of work did he do? No work yet. What did he want to do? He didn't know. He was fond of the Finnish girls, he said, and they of him. He loved Finland. This was home. He would never, he said, with a shrug and no perceptible emotion, never live in Somalia again.

WHY PUTIN IS STILL IN POWER

Moscow-St. Petersburg, Russia

I walked into one of the many casinos that dot the city to see what was going on, maybe join a card game.

As I walked in, it was dark, and there wasn't a lot of action. Six guys were sitting at a tournament-style poker table, but nobody was dealing. Where chips and cards should have been, each had an open laptop. They were playing on a poker website and sharing information with each other, trimming whoever was unfortunate enough to end up playing with them. These guys looked up at me a bit like I was the neighbor's cat, just happening to walk by. They didn't seem to like or particularly dislike cats. They just weren't interested in cats.

Their body language made it clear that they were working and didn't want a hello, much less a chat. I pretended to check out one of the slot machines, and they continued to talk through their strategy with each other, figuring out the best way to take the money off whatever hapless sod in Idaho or Costa Rica sat down at their cybertable. This kind of criminal conspiracy was not something they thought they had to hide even a little.

I walked back out, the night calming the streets down to a trickle. It was beginning to be time not to be on the streets.

Yes, there is a McDonalds next to Lenin's tomb in Moscow, and yes, there is a chain of fast-food blini places in the major cities. But one can walk down block after block of downtown St. Petersburg and not find a single business establishment. So, when walking back to my apartment, I saw a crowd gathered outside one of the few restaurants in the neighborhood, I went to see what the fuss was about.

It turned out to be a gleaming red Ferrari, parked while the owner, presumably, was eating. The admiration people had for this car, and the schoolgirl- and schoolboylike excitement of the crowd had waiting for whoever the oligarch was to come back and drive it away—why? Do they not see this guy as part of the problem? What kind of fantasy solution does the Ferrari represent? Of the forty people gathered, maybe one or two owned a car at all. None were friends of Putin's. Yet they loved this as yet unseen oligarch like people love movie stars, and they hung on his return. I suppose in the age of Trump I should have been less surprised.

Much later that night, around 11 PM, as I was heading home from a late dinner, two young women came by riding horses on the sidewalk. They were upper-middle-class girls, it seemed to me, maybe twenty or twenty-one, and I said hello, hoping at least one of them spoke some English. They pulled to a stop, and one girl said hello.

Why are you riding horses in the city? I asked.

Give me some money, she said.

Excuse me?

Give me some money for my horse, she said. The other girl just watched her, straight-faced.

Why? I asked. Why would I give you money?

For my horse, she said. Give me money.

It's 11 PM, I said. Why are you riding horses in the city in the middle of the night?

Are you going to give me money? she said more than asked, a bit peevish now.

No, I said, I'm not going to give you money.

Fuck you, she said, gave her horse a little kick, and the two of them cantered off into the night.

THE PAINTED CROSSES OF MARAMUREŞ
Săpânţa, Romania

In Sighetu Marmaţiei, in the far north of Romania, I had spent a day
of death visiting the Jewish cemetery and Elie Wiesel's house, which
documents the destruction of the area's Jews over a few months in
1944.

Not a mile out of town I came across another cemetery. This one
was on fire. It was an overcast day, with the clouds close to the earth.
In an overgrown field of ornate black metal crosses, surrounded
by a black iron, filigreed fence, flames were shooting fitfully out of
smoldering piles of cuttings, thick smoke snaking across the road. I
braked, turned around, and parked. The groundskeepers had hacked
away great swaths of brush, which were now burning in a dozen piles
while they continued to trim. The smoke and streaks of flame filled
the cemetery with B-movie portentousness and obscured the grave
markers, all of which were short crosses with a small black metal
plate, the name and dates of the deceased hand-lettered in white
paint. It looked more like a Great War–era battlefield graveyard than
a permanent memorial, and the markers seemed more quickly des-
tined to oblivion than even the soft stones in the Jewish cemetery
in Sighet, most of which were unreadable. It made me wonder about
local customs—was there an incredibly successful brochure that
read, For your loved one, you'll want the Simple Iron Cross Model?
The thing that surprised me was that these were not markers from

World War I, despite their late Victorian look. Every one I checked was from the 1990s or later. How do these modes of memorialization spring up? Where do they come from? Who, exactly, invents the new traditions?

I found one answer at my next cemetery, another fifteen miles west. In 1935, in the town of Săpânţa, a man named Stan IoanPătraş began fashioning wooden grave markers, carved in bas-relief, which he then painted. He continued making them until his death in 1977; since then his apprentice, Dumitru Pop, has continued. Each marker is a wooden structure eight feet tall, and each has, at the center, a picture of the deceased, carved in bas-relief, and a poem, often ironic, using bits of local dialect.

On the back Pătraş and Pop carved another picture and painted the whole thing in bright tempera colors, including a distinctive blue, dubbed Săpânţa blue. Each marker is topped with an a equilateral cross with round terminals and then by a small roof, more like a peaked six-inch-wide rafter, with a tin covering that keeps the most obvious problem of weathering at bay and adds to the complexity of the image. The result is the most colorful graveyard in Europe, nicknamed the Merry Cemetery. The markers have a Grandma Moses feel, eschewing painterly conventions of perspective and technique, and yet with a coherent aesthetic—that combination of guilelessness and gusto that makes folk craft into folk art.

The central images of the deceased are often pointedly traditional, with a woman spinning wool or literally stirring a pot in the kitchen, farmers in the field, or men otherwise at their jobs—a bartender, a shepherd, a woodsman—but with striking bits of modernity, the brand name of the tractor, for instance, or a fruit grower spraying his trees with insecticide. They often manage to evoke a very specific person with a single detail, like a logger's account book or a pharmacist's glasses. A butcher, for instance, is shown in his shop, with his cleaver, a string of carcasses in the "background"—although background isn't quite right, again, given the lack of perspective—scales for weighing, a purse slung over his shoulder for selling, and then a surprisingly large meerschaum pipe sticking out of his mouth, transforming him from a generic to an individual butcher. On another, a military man seems to be commanding his troops, but because of the flattened perspective it isn't clear whether his troops' guns and bayonets point away or face him; the man comes alive as you ponder this.

An example of the memorial poetry from one of the markers (translations from Wikipedia):

> Under this heavy cross
> Lays my poor mother in-law
> Three more days she would have lived
> I would lay, and she would read [this cross].
> You, who here are passing by
> Not to wake her up please try
> For if she comes back home
> She'll criticize me more.

Calling Henny Youngman, Pătraș wants his mother-in-law joke back. This is the one that everyone in Romania knows and can give you a version of—though the three days is sometimes one day and sometimes gets reduced to an hour.
One marker says:

> IoanToaderu loved horses.
> One more thing he loved very much.
> To sit at a table in a bar.
> Next to someone else's wife.

Here is Pătraș's own epigraph:

De cu tînăr copilaş	Since I was a little boy
Io am fost Stan Ion Pătraş	I was known as Stan Ioan Pătraş
Să mă ascultaţ oameni buni	Listen to me, fellows
Ce voi spune nu-s minciuni	There are no lies in what I am
	going to say
Cîte zile am trăit	
Rău la nime n-am dorit	All along my life
Dar bine cît-am putut	I meant no harm to anyone
Orişicine mia cerut	But did good as much as I could
	To anyone who asked
Vai săraca lumea mea	
Că greu am trăit în ea	Oh, my poor World
	Because It was hard living in it

On the back of many of Pătraş and Pop's markers is an image of the deceased's mode of death. A woman gets hit by a car, forever. A ten-year-old boy, who was run over by a bus, graphically if impossibly is having his legs completely flattened by the back wheels of the bus while the rest of him, upright, looks out at the viewer with a straight face.

A few people refuse to go with the crowd. The grave of a guy named Pop Turder (1905–1990) has a gray stone, rather than a wooden marker, inset with a photograph of himself in traditional Hungarian costume. Stan Ion (Huciu) (I don't know why the last name is in parentheses—1907–2001) lies under marble, again with a photo, as if these two were purposely indicting photography as an inferior art, unable to compete with even a marginally skillful painter.

Perhaps, though, these two worried about longevity; a few of the earliest markers have lost all their paint. Perhaps they were just wealthy and wanted people to know it. But the other cemeteries in Maramureş, with plenty of graves like theirs, stand empty, seldom visited, while Pătraş and Pop's graveyard has a steady stream, almost as many live people as dead, day in and day out.

Pătraş and Pop have found, in their little cemetery shop, the vast consolation of art and have stolen at least a little chill from the grave.

WAITING AT THE BULGARIAN BORDER

East of Delchevo, Macedonia

At the Macedonian border with Bulgaria, we started to collect. The several truck drivers seemed more relaxed than the rest of us—they had been through this before. A family in several cars, each with an enormous wrapped load on the roof, kept to themselves. Three men of various ages who didn't seem to match, and had perhaps just met, were talking closely near the immigration booth. An hour turned into two, the crowd grew larger. Computer problems, the immigration agent explained from his booth as, flustered, he kept opening and closing desk drawers, occasionally punching his keyboard, walking back and forth to the main office, trying to look like he was doing something. But, he said, shrugging, the problem was in Sofia, there was nothing he could do.

I began a conversation with one of the three mismatched men. He was, indeed, traveling with the other two, although he was the only one who spoke English. As we talked the other two wandered off. He was Romanian and had never had trouble with this border.

Still, he said, I am Romanian. I have experience waiting in lines. He looked to be in his thirties.

So you remember the Ceauşescu regime?

Of course! he said. I remember being hungry, it is not something you forget.

He was twelve, he told me, when the 1989 revolution happened, and had a lot of strong memories.

Lines for bread, he said. Lines for medicine, lines for shoes, if there were shoes. But then, at the end, there were not even lines. On a streetcar in the winter, in only a light shirt, I remember shivering, trying to decide whether to hold on to the icy metal rail with my bare hand in the wind or hug myself and risk getting thrown out of the car. You cannot imagine how bad it was.

Because of the spying, the repression too? I asked. I had seen Ceauşescu's palace, the Versailles-like excess, had heard the stories of the secret police, assassination, torture.

Maybe some people worried about those things, he said. But no, I was young, and when things got very bad, I don't know how anyone could worry about the police. We had been reduced to animals, we needed everything. All we could think was to find something to eat. Our days were trying to find food. Picking through garbage, that was not the worst. Scraping at the frozen ground for roots.

There was movement near the passport booth. The computer was back up.

This is Bulgaria, he said. That was not a bad wait.

He was a minister, he told me, for a nondenominational Christian church. His father had been a minister too, but of course there was no religion allowed during the Ceauşescu years.

He had just been on a missionary trip to Macedonia. I asked him whether he was happy with Romania now.

Happy? Yes, he said, although his face said otherwise, still perhaps remembering scraping that frozen ground. He looked up at me, the adult minister doing its best to assert itself over the haunted boy, and forced a smile. The past will not come back, he said. And this is good.

He didn't sound completely confident.

HOLDING A GRUDGE

Upper Town, Gibraltar

He was a native of Gibraltar, as were his father and his father's father, and he had lived on the rock for all of his seventy-six years. He made disparaging remarks about the Spanish.

You don't like your neighbors? I asked. I expected him to say the normal things—there are good ones and bad ones, people are the same everywhere.

They are the most deceiving, dastardly, bloodthirsty villains on earth! he said, with great heat, and a little spit. It was the first time I heard someone use dastardly without irony. He had long, grizzly sideburns, not quite muttonchops, but close.

His friend, a less fiery sixty-year-old, agreed.

Yah, we hate 'em.

Really! And is that a common feeling, here? I asked.

What do you expect? the older man said. We've been at war since the beginning of time.

At war? Literally? They both nodded yes. I thought that was over and settled ages ago, I said.

Not at all! Muttonchops said. They would like nothing better than to get rid of us, and they'd stop at nothing. Our defenses are the only reason they haven't done it already.

Is that right! I said. I had no idea.

Ah, they're nasty buggers, the Spanish, said the calm one.

And do they feel that way about you?

I wouldn't know, would I? he said.

The country has the feeling of an island, though it's a peninsula. The border with Spain has at times been closed completely—the longest period recently being from 1969 to 1985—and when tensions are high, which they often are, customs inspectors on both sides of the border inspect every car, and lines are three and four hours long. It is tiny. The only countries or territories that are smaller are Monaco, the Vatican, and four islands. The famous rock takes up most of the peninsula, and almost half the flats is claimed by the airport. You have to cross the runway to drive in from Spain, and another queue forms ten times a day when a plane takes off or lands.

You know they've put us under siege, Muttonchops said. Over and over again, literally tried to starve us to death.

No! I felt that I would have heard something. When was this? I asked.

The last time? Muttonchops said, thinking.

It has happened many times, his friend said.

Yes, that is what I'm telling him! Is he daft? he asked his friend, rhetorically, about me.

Okay, then, yes, the most recent, I said.

Well, let's see, he said, looking at his quieter friend, whose look admitted he would be no help. That would be 1782, am I right? 1783.

His friend nodded ominously, confirming—that sounded right to him. He looked at me with a challenge.

Yes, that's right, he said, 1783.

They both looked fighting mad about it. Muttonchops emerged from his slightly cross-eyed ruminations to look at me bitterly. Perhaps, he had started to think, perhaps I was on the side of the enemy.

BUSINESS LUNCH

Downtown Minsk, Belarus

A woman about fifty or so, very vigorous, saw me struggling with the menu and offered to help. She was blond and bright-eyed, with an easy smile, in a business skirt and jacket. She was with a friend, five or ten years younger, also dressed for the office, both with full makeup and scarves, out for lunch in the middle of their workday.

Don't use this, she said, dismissing the dusty, crumbling twenty-page English menu the waiter had given me. This—pointing at a card on the table that had the day's specials—is much better prices. She walked me through the options—it was all the same, as it turned out, just a matter of choosing the stuffing in the potato pancake, so whatever she said, I just went ahead and said, good, yes, that.

You would like to drink? Cognac, whiskey? It was just before noon.

Wine?

Red? What country?

Belarus?

No, she said, with a quick look to the heavens and a hand to her chest. I am a patriot, but I cannot allow this.

The waiter was standing by, and she was giving him my order. She explained to him that I had asked for Belarusian wine. He looked slightly to my left and shook his head sadly.

France, Chile, Italy, she suggested.

Chile, I said.

Chile, she said to the waiter, who had already eye-checked his approval and was writing it down. They looked at each other and agreed—if he likes Chilean wine, then he would have hated Belarusian.

I thanked her profusely, and she gave me an *aw shucks* gesture.

Really, not at all, she said, I saw you struggling, and giving a dismissive gesture to the menu, she added: They don't even give you Russian menu!

I wasn't sure why that was a bad thing. She sat back down at the booth across from my table, and we continued talking.

They spoke some English because they worked in international banking. The friend was tongue-tied and said something Belarusian. My translator said: We know banking language, we can do everything on the phone for business, but she is afraid of speaking.

Once I get started, she said, I will be okay.

There! I said. You're started! She blushed and said barely another word of English until the check came, but she seemed to understand everything we were saying.

Here! the blond said. You are stranger and I am translator, you come and eat with us.

I thanked them and climbed into their booth. Our drinks arrived—their two generous snifters of cognac and my wine. We clinked glasses and I said one of my seventeen words of Russian, *nas'trovya.*

They wanted to know where I was from, why I had come to Belarus, whether my ancestors were from Belarus, what I had seen. I told them I had been to Polach, Vitsebsk, Mir, the lakes in the northwest.

They wanted to know how I knew which buses to take, and I said no, no buses, I drove.

Just with map? she asked. When I said yes, they had a colloquy, and then she turned back to me. We are saying you are most impressive tourist, she said. You have no reason to be here. You don't speak Russian but you go everywhere in the country. No English in the provinces, yes?

Yes, no English, I laughed. But it is easy to get what you need. I mimed putting food in my mouth, then the palms-up, arms-akimbo international sign for "where?" And the international sign for going to sleep, head to the side on my hands, eyes closed. And, I added, everyone has a calculator to show you how much to pay.

You are brave man, anyway, she said. Because I know, the governments of U.S., U.K., Germany—if you read their reports, it is very scary here, very dangerous. But you see! she said, holding out her hands, it is not! All the advertising we get is about crazy Lukashenko . . .

Alexander Lukashenko has been president of Belarus since 1994 and has kept the country hewing closer to the old Soviet Union style than even the Russian Federation. Called Europe's "Last Dictator," he had term limits eliminated, has complete control over the legislature and all government spending, and has been sanctioned by both the United States and the European Union for human rights abuses. He is unfazed by the international condemnation. "The history of Germany is a copy of the history of Belarus," Lukashenko said in 1995. "Germany was raised from ruins thanks to firm authority and not everything connected with that well-known figure Hitler was bad. German order evolved over the centuries and attained its peak under Hitler." And in 2012, after a meeting in Brussels rebuked him for violence against and repression of the LGBT community, his only comment was, "it is better to be a dictator than gay."

Yes, Lukashenko, I said—I had learned it makes sense to try a positive statement to initiate political discussions in such places. He seems to be taking care of the economy. I see building going on everywhere, everything is so clean—

Always this place is clean, she said, brusque, the insistence holding both pride and something else, defensiveness? Ever since I was a girl it is clean!

Not just that, I said, the roads are excellent, great infrastructure, much better than America.

Yes, well, Lukashenko. Always I was the opposite, she said, meaning part of the opposition. And I think Lukashenko is ignorant. And that he thinks always about himself, like all politicians. But I now think his heart is not all bad, and he wants what is best for Belarus.

So has Belarus changed much in your lifetime? I asked. Did the separation from Moscow change things very much?

No, not in the heart, she said, fist to chest. It is the same, the people the same, the life the same. Of course, like everywhere, everything is changed, computers, but no, this is the same place as when I was a girl.

When I was in Ukraine, I said, and in Latvia, I met Russians who wanted their countries back in the Russian Federation. Are there people here who want that?

No, nobody here wants to be Russia. We are really more Poland than Russia. People say to me, "hey, you are not like typical Russian," and I say, of course! I am not Russian!

She was a patriot, very proud of Belarus.

Forty percent of our people make their living from their brains, she said at one point. We have our own high-tech park, like Silicon Valley, and we make programmers for the whole world—my nephew is in Los Angeles as programmer, my brother in Germany. Forty percent! Think of this. With their—and she points to her head—forty percent!

So you are happy here.

Can't you tell? she said, with a laugh. I don't want to leave here, why leave? I work, I don't believe my work would be different someplace else, would it? International banking is international. I am happy here, yes. If it got dangerous, I would leave, of course, but no, I love it here.

I told her about going to a small bookstore, called Ў—pronounced *eu*, and not exactly a y, ў is known as the Belarusian letter; it is not in the Russian alphabet. I told her that I was quite impressed by the interesting little magazines, literary journals—it seems like a vibrant intellectual culture.

Yes, but here in Minsk only. In the provinces, not at all.

So who is the best writer?

Oh! she said. Write this down! Svetlana Alexievich! She is the best. Also, Vassil Bykov, he died just three years ago or so, he is a classic. That is enough for you to start, those two.

Alexievich would win the Nobel Prize for Literature a month later.

And do you have a film industry?

Yes, she said. But it is not good, it is like Russian film—everything shoot, kill.

I am a fan of Romanian film, does that come here?

I don't know, I don't know it. But there is Yugoslav director—and she turned to her friend and gave some titles, I assume. The friend shrugged. Ah, I can't think of his name, she said, but he is like Tarantino, very good.

So you get American film.

Everywhere, she said and rolled her eyes. American film is everywhere. She looked at me, as if she might have overestimated me—who doesn't know that American film is everywhere?—and made no further comment.

When the check came I offered to pick up theirs, and the friend said, no, no, and grabbed the two checks the waiter had left and handed me mine.

I insist, I said, please, you have been so kind.

The blond took their check from her friend and handed it to me.

Yes! she said. He can pay! I am his interpreter! and she laughed.

But I didn't help! the friend said, reaching for her wallet.

I am happy to treat you, I said. Truly.

You see I am very shy! the blond said, patting her friend's hand to put her wallet away. And, of course, she said, her attention back to me, we are kind, as you say. But now, we must go back to work. We must help keep Belarus's infrastructure so excellent!

We each did the three-cheek kiss and they walked away, making a joke with the waiter, about leaving the check with me I assume. He came over, still smiling—it was a good joke, apparently—and I ordered a coffee. Coffee is one of the most international words—the o gets rounder or flatter, but the rest stays the same. Like kindness, it is easy for everyone to recognize.

BEING JEWISH IN BELARUS

Minsk International Airport, Belarus

In the Minsk airport, I misplaced my phone. I had been dozing on and off during a horrible delay, and when I patted my pockets to find it, it was gone. I methodically went through every one of the forty-five pockets in my pack, patted all my pockets again, and refused to let myself panic. I tried everywhere a third time.

I decided it was, in fact, gone. I retraced my steps to a couch I had napped on, and three middle-aged women looked up at me. They said something I took to be asking what I was looking for.

My phone! I said, having seen billboards for a new СМАРТФОН, or smartphone, along the highway. Smartphone, I said.

Ah! They jumped up, and one took me by the arm—they had clearly found it and handed it in—and marched me across the terminal.

Where are you from? she asked.

Los Angeles.

Ah! she said, and pulled back her jacket to show the *Herbalife* insignia on her shiny green and black jumpsuit, and pointing to her friends, wearing the same suits, and herself. We work for Los Angeles! In Vladivostok. It was a three-hour flight to Moscow, she told me, and then nine hours to Vladivostok.

She brought me to an information booth where my guide explained that the phone she had handed in a few minutes earlier was mine. Only one of the three older women in the booth looked up

at us, and she transferred us to a young, dark-haired woman, perhaps
because she had better English, or perhaps it was just her turn—or
perhaps because she was the youngest, so it was always her turn.

What kind of phone? she asked, suspiciously.

An iPhone, I said.

What color? again, unaccountably distrustful. I wondered how
many iPhones had been lost that day, and it slowed me down. Also, it
was white but had a black cover. I hesitated.

You have to know what color it is to get the phone, she said, as if I
was some kind of thief. You must go to Lost and Found, downstairs,
near Gate 5-6, she said. Then she looked back at some papers, done
with us.

I thanked the woman from Herbalife, who was very sweet and gave
my hand a warm squeeze. I went downstairs, dragging all my gear,
and found Gate 1-2, then Gate 3-4, then an unmarked gate, then the
end of the terminal. I went back to other end to see if 5-6 was over
there; it wasn't. I came back to the unmarked gate, stuck my head in
and asked if it was the lost and found department. A fit, gray-haired
man with a metal-detecting wand pointed upstairs. I said that they
had told me downstairs. A quick survey was taken of the three or
four people hanging around, and nobody spoke English. Go, he said,
meaning come, and strode away. I followed him back to the information booth upstairs. The sour young woman looked unhappy to see
us.

The Lost and Found is lost, I said.

Did you go to Gate 5-6? she said, this time like a fed-up schoolteacher.

I think so, I said, pointing to the guy, but he was already headed
back.

You have to go outside to get to 5-6, she said, like everyone knew
that, and I was being obstinate. One of the older women barked at her
and she let out a poof of disapproval and stood up. She walked me to
the elevator, saying nothing, got in, and though she was closer to the
buttons, said, one, imperious. I pushed the button. We went down
and outside, and I asked if she had been born in Minsk.

What?

You were born in Minsk?

Of course.

In the city?

No, a hundred kilometers west. Babruysk. Very Jewish town.

Now? I asked. It is Jewish now?

Yes, she said.

I was wondering if there were any Jews here anymore, I said, and she didn't say anything.

The day before, I had gone downtown, parked at the corner of Marx and Lenin boulevards and walked over to the Museum of Belarusian Culture. It did not have a single trace of the Jews who had once made up more than 50 percent of the population of Minsk and other large towns. I even watched a forty-five-minute film about World War II at the museum, and it had not a single mention of Jews. A quarter of the Jews in Belarus escaped, and the Germans and the Belorussian police murdered more than half during the war. Of those left, the majority had emigrated by 1990. They now represent less than a half a percent of the population.

We had arrived at lost and found. My phone was on a desk. I pointed at it, and the woman handed it to me without question. The young woman from Babruysk was already leaving, but I caught up with her as we made our way back upstairs.

So are you Jewish, then? I asked

She took a moment.

If it will help me, I am Jewish. If it will not—she shrugged. She didn't look directly at me through any of this.

I wanted to ask someone, I said, so let me ask you. At the Museum of Belarusian Culture, I watched a film about the Great Patriotic War, and Jews were never mentioned. There was nothing about Jews in the whole museum. Pictures of old Minsk, old cities, but no Jews any-where.

No? She seemed unsurprised and unmoved.

And I saw no synagogue.

Yes, I think there is no synagogue in Minsk.

But in your town?

Oh, yes. It is very Jewish, 90 percent Jewish, it is only place where even the Russians speak Jewish.

It wasn't 90 percent, I found later, but maybe more than half.

They speak Yiddish, or Hebrew?

Yes, Jewish. Still, now, some speak Jewish.

And so tell me, is there anti-Semitism now in Belarus?

No! she said, but with a slight smile.

Really? Because it is everywhere in Europe now—France, Hungary, Greece—but not here?

No, she said, and stepped back in her booth.

I tipped my hat to the klatch. They all gave a brief professional smile and went back to chatting.

I have no idea whether she was Jewish.

At the security gate, the woman checking my passport, around thirty-five or forty, hair dyed dark red, said, as she handed me back my passport, Los Angeles California! Hollywood! Say hello to Madonna for me!

Okay, I said, I will, and smiled. Anyone else in Hollywood I can say hello to for you?

No, she said, very excited. Just Madonna. I love Madonna. Today! Today Madonna starts new show, Rebel Gull! Today!

ACKNOWLEDGMENTS

Many thanks to Carl Klaus and Elisabeth Chretien at University of Iowa Press for taking this on, and to Carolyn Brown for saving me countless times. Thanks to the usual suspects: Paul Mandelbaum, Jon Wiener, and Seth Greenland, and to Janet Fitch, Juan Felipe Herrera, and Laila Lalami for reading the galleys. To Jamie Wolf, Albert Litewka, and the rest of the board of the *Los Angeles Review of Books,* to all my co-conspirators there, and to my fellow travelers, those who have shared the road with me. As always, too: Jesse, Yarrow, Cody, Guillermo, Ken, April, Mayela, and Laurie Winer: first reader, best reader; or, as she says, her first, my last.

Photographs from these journeys can be viewed at OntheRoofof theWorld.com.

SIGHTLINE BOOKS

The Iowa Series in Literary Nonfiction